Surviving Digital

The 7-Step Digital Marketing Strateg
On The High Street And Online

By Viv Craske

Praise for Surviving Digital Disruption:

"The world is dividing into companies that innovate and those being disrupted. In this knowledge age, entrepreneurs need to understand digital marketing as it offers unprecedented reach and power. Businesses that fail to adapt will be lucky to survive at all. This book shows how retailers and food brands can survive the disruption and thrive as they emerge into the digital age."
Daniel Priestley, best-selling author of Oversubscribed, Entrepreneur Revolution and Key Person of Influence; CEO, Dent

"The biggest challenge with getting digital right in the FMCG industry is that the rule book hasn't been written. Surviving Digital Disruption means this is no longer a viable excuse! An essential read for any FMCG professional."
Stuart Heffernan, E-commerce Trading Controller, GSK

Copyright: Viv Craske 2016. Cover design by Moniq Silva – www.vexalist.com

Contents

Introduction	Page 6
Overcoming Too Much Choice, Too Much Noise	Page 10
Step 1: What is Digital Shopper Marketing? Defining The Role Of Digital	Page 30
Step 2: Owning The Path To Purchase	Page 60
Step 3: Hacking The In-Store Experience	Page 89
Step 4: Jail-Breaking E-Commerce: Freeing Sales From Its Desktop Prison	Page 140
Step 5: Post-Purchase: Creating Digital Advocates	Page 167
Step 6: Hacking The Brief	Page 201
Step 7: Six Blind Men And An Elephant: Killing The Silos And Dogma That Cause Your Team To Fail	Page 213
Amazon's Killer Terminators	Page 231

About The Author

Viv Craske is an entrepreneurial marketer and digital evangelist. He is interested in ideas at the intersection of food, technology and people. His heroes are industry disrupters who focus on making the world a little bit better.

Viv had a previous career as a magazine editor, working on the world's biggest dance music and clubbing magazine, *Mixmag*. He has debated UK recreational drug policy on *Newsnight*, studied to become a qualified hypnotherapist, and has a biochemistry degree. He set up the UK's first full-service boutique social media agency. He was a *Masterchef* contestant, making kedgeree and Thai curry.

Viv lives in Brighton, England with his wife and two children. His wife runs a business baking Swedish cakes and Viv tries to not get fat eating the leftovers.

How To Get The Most From This Book

This book is written for a specific audience: marketers for retailers and FMCG brands.

You can read the book in a linear fashion (recommended), as the initial chapters set up the strategy and thinking that make the tactics in later chapters easier to understand.

There are also chapters that are of more importance for you, depending on your business sector.

At the end of every chapter are summary bullet points and Jobs To Be Done, which I hope will become a handy reference guide for implementing the ideas in this book.

Hello FMCG marketers…

If you're a CMO, brand manager, shopper manager, head of digital, CDO or CIO at an FMCG brand, the majority of this book is written with you in mind.

Step 2: Owning The Path To Purchase is a key chapter for those working with FMCG brands, as we look at the challenges of who owns the shopper relationship – the FMCG brand or the retailers? – and how to tip relationships in your favour.

Hello retail marketers…

If you're a CMO, COO, head of retail, head of digital, CDO or CIO at a multiple High Street or big box retailer, the majority of this book is also written for you. The following chapters might be an interesting place to dive straight in:

Step 3: Hacking The In-Store Experience

Step 4: Jail-Breaking E-Commerce: Freeing Your Sales From Its Desktop Prison

Hello all marketers…

While many of the examples in this book are taken from UK campaigns and brands, I hope that the ideas given in this book also have value beyond the UK. In many ways, the UK market can lag behind the US, Europe and now Asia in terms of digital marketing, but in other ways, many still look to the UK for best-in-class activations and the quality of our marketing.

While the focus of this book is FMCG brands and retailers, I hope that there are ideas and inspiration that translates to luxury, entertainment and leisure sector brands. Ultimately, I hope there is value for any marketer who is focused on improving their digital thinking.

As marketers, we're essentially telling stories about our brands that we hope will resonate with shoppers and consumers. The ideas in this book may help you tell better stories and, when integrating digital, help to tell stories even better.

Introduction

When I was 16 I had a Saturday job at a branch of Tesco in Yeovil, Somerset. It was in the days before barcode scanning, and I didn't like my job very much, so when products lost their price sticker, I just used to guess and type in a price that I imagined was in the rough ballpark of whatever was on the conveyer belt. I was a terrible checkout assistant.

One Saturday, my supervisor asked me if I could fill in a survey from head office. The one question I remember asked: "Do you think Tesco customers would prefer to be served by an efficient robot or a friendly human?" I was a grumpy teenager and hated the monotony of sitting on the tills.

I ticked the box on the form that said "efficient robot".

Later that day, my supervisor stopped by my till to have a quick word.

"You've written the incorrect answer here," she said, pointing to the robot question. "Here's a pen;, please change it so I can send these forms off to head office today."

"I'm sorry, I can't," I said. "That's really what I think. If you wanted me to write the other answer, you shouldn't have given me a choice."

"Well, this is going to look bad on you and me," she said, and took the form back and walked away.

The problem was, I didn't care. I didn't care about the customers. I didn't care about Tesco. I wasn't invested in anything other than my hourly wage. I was working at a Saturday job that, at first, earned me just over £15 a week. I did the job because it was easy to get, easy to do and paid me beer money. It was purely transactional. And from my 16-year-old standpoint, I felt my attitude was absolutely fine. I was swapping my time for money, and Tesco swapped tins and ready meals for money. That was all there was to retailing. Why should I care about Tesco or the products we sold or our customers?

Years later I got it.

I got why we care about supermarkets.

I got that the kitchen and the dinner table is the heart of the home and the heart needs a constant supply of groceries – and where you buy your groceries is not just about price and convenience, but what that choice of retailer says about the values you have for yourself and your family.

Of course customers didn't want a robot. They wanted excellent service, great value; they wanted shopping to be easy… maybe even fun. They wanted the retailers and its staff to care about them.

The world faces disruption of the financial system. The disruption of how we work. Technology and AI is set to make many jobs redundant. Retail has moved from High Street stores to e-commerce marketplaces. Large FMCG brands have digital and innovation incubators, while anybody can fund their new food brand on Kickstarter.

While this digital disruption is happening around us, we have our day-to-day work to do as marketers. Looming deadlines and limited resources can drive our thinking. We are expected to do more with less, to spread our budgets across a splintering range of touchpoints. Our shoppers and consumers see more adverts than ever, and online ad response rates have been declining for years.

It's this state of disruption that keeps many businesses from disrupting themselves. New businesses disrupt the retail market, and everyone else catches up.

To many people it was obvious that music retail was going to move from selling CDs to selling digital files in the late 90s and early 00s. And while HMV and record companies made some steps in the direction of selling music online, they moved slowly, dragging piles of red tape and business dogma behind them. It took Apple's iTunes to disrupt the market and steal a large slice of the market share.

Existing large taxi firms could have seen the early potential of Uber and Lyft and created their own app-based business. But the industry resisted change and focused on public protests and legal challenges instead.

Since late 2014, I have been warning UK FMCG brands and food retailers about the disruption that Amazon is going to cause. But many seem to have a "wait and see" attitude.

Without wanting to be alarmist, you need to disrupt your industry or be disrupted. Digital is driving much of the disruption in our industry. If you want to be on the High Street and thriving online five years from now, you need to start welcoming and adapting to the digital changes happening in retail and FMCG marketing.

There's a Japanese word – *kaizen* – that can be translated as never-ending constant improvement. The world has changed. What worked yesterday might not work today or tomorrow. We need to constantly improve our marketing. That means creating digital marketing strategies and campaigns that work better than that of our competitors.

This book is both a rallying cry and a how-to guide to become the disrupter in your company. If at any time reading this book, you have a question or comment about how to make the changes you want, feel free to email me on: viv@vivcraske.com

Overcoming Too Much Choice, Too Much Noise

My Dad, John Craske, ran a local grocery store in the 1940s in Cornwall. I love hearing my dad talk about his time running the store. To me it seems like a magical time, before the birth of the modern supermarket in the UK, before the power of TV advertising and before the power of branded products.

Customer service was everything.

And marketing, of course, was much simpler.

The path to purchase used to be easy. You advertised your product to the widest possible audience, and reminded them in store by having it displayed on the shelf. The local shopkeeper bought what he thought were the best products for his shoppers, and what they asked him for.

Biscuits came in large tins and sweets in glass jars, to be weighed and sold in paper bags – gob-stoppers for a penny and four chews for a penny. Dad's general store was opposite the village school and sold a lot of sweets.

In the store, my dad cut bacon from the side. It was boned by hand and cut in joints to order, with rashers cut to customers' preference for thickness, by hand, then as Dad invested further in his business, by a hand-turned bacon slicer.

Lard came in large wooden boxes and had to be weighed and wrapped in 8 and 16oz greaseproof paper packets. Saffron came in 1lb tins and had to be sold in 16 one-dram packets. Eggs were loose, from the tray. Twist tobacco came on a roll and was sold by the yard. One man arrived at 7.30am five mornings a week for his packet of 10 Woodbines. The baker from nearby Wadebridge delivered fresh bread six days a week.

They offered whatever services the local community needed. Dad sold weekly newspapers and magazines and comics, but also paraffin for stoves, filling from the tank out the back. Brake pads and new tyres were fitted onto bikes, along with chains that had come off their cogs, all for a small charge (and sometimes free to kids). They took in shoe repairs, collected by repairers from the town and returned a week later.

When talking to my dad, two key themes come through. 1) A "smell what sells" approach, and 2) A strong desire to serve the local community – because it makes good business sense, but also because they were an integral part of the local community – and who doesn't like helping out their friends and neighbours?

The best example of customer service Dad talks about is his approach to presents. He brought in possible birthday and Christmas presents, as well as cards with individual customers in mind. He knew what his customers and their families liked and he made sure he had something suitable in stock as their key calendar dates approached. At Christmas, Dad and his wife made and decorated his own Christmas cakes, and in season, bottled peaches in syrup.

Dad also understood the importance of home delivery and Sunday shopping, even in the 1940s. On Fridays, Dad delivered to customers' doors. And while Sunday trading laws meant that stores couldn't open on Sundays, if you ran out of something, you could always go to the back door of Dad's shop and home and Dad would always get you what you needed.

Dad joined the business when his father was rushed to hospital. He learned and took over the trade, and over time helped to form a local co-operative with other local traders. He became the president of the North Cornwall Grocers Association in his thirties. By that time, he was running two, and for a time, three village shops that would have been too small to be profitable alone.

What's interesting for me is that many of the current trends the major grocery retailers are focused on are very old ideas that shopkeepers like my dad were practising in the 1940s: dedication to customer service; ranges targeted to the local area, home delivery…

The biggest difference is that in listening to my dad's stories, he never once mentions brands. They just didn't exist until TV allowed them to exist, and until increasing travel meant that national brands could create some kind of consistency and brand equity.

The Path To Purchase

The rise of the supermarket gave birth to brand marketing, which of course led to the importance of mass market TV advertising, coining the phrase "from sofa to store".

The world used to be simple. You came home to your dinner in front of the telly and you saw an ad for a brand of fish fingers. If the ad had an emotional impact on you, that meant you liked the product and remembered the brand, you'd add fish fingers to your shopping list and next time you drove or took the bus to the supermarket, you remembered the brand when you were in the freezer aisle and you bought it.

The path to purchase was simple.

Brand awareness ---> Purchase consideration ---> Trial/Purchase
(TV)   (TV)   (In store)

Sure, I am oversimplifying things, I know. Maybe there were print ads and radio ads too. Maybe there was an ad on a billboard or a bus stop. Maybe even a shelf edge barker in the freezer aisle offering a price discount.

It was still simple because, in general, there was a single path to purchase that marketers and brands could visualize and focus on. Sofa. Telly. Store.

And then the world got busy with ads.

And then the internet changed everything.

And then e-commerce changed everything.

And then social media changed everything.

And now mobile is about to change everything.

And now digital in store media is going to change everything.

And this proliferation of channels, media and touchpoints, combined with the existing print options, mean that people can take a variety of routes to travel along a path to purchase from brand awareness to sale.

That path could be:

TV ---> Facebook ---> Billboard ---> Twitter ---> Online ad ---> E-commerce

Or it could be:

Mobile offer ---> Instagram ---> Online video ---> Bus stop sign ---> ATM ad ---> Barker in store

Or it could be any combination of owned, earned and paid media in any and all channels, touchpoints and media.

And it might not even be a path to purchase in the sense of a linear path. It might be looping or fragmented. It could look as straight as an arrow. Or it could look like a messy ball of wool that a kitten has been playing with.

And it could be a different path for huge numbers of different shoppers.

And when the shopper is not always the same person as the consumer, it could be a combination of different paths to purchase with a little moment of word of mouth linking them together.

Or it could be that I've been on one path to purchase to get me interested in a new brand of fish fingers and added them to my online grocery cart. A few days later, my partner sees them in the cart and buys them – or not, depending on how he or she has been influenced as a shopper toward or away from that same brand and product on his or her own path to purchase.

When I sit down to talk about these issues with brand managers and agency planners, other digital people and account management people, it's easy to wonder how we as an industry ever manage to focus on defining the most important paths to purchase.

No one has *the* answer – as in, all the answers – but in working with our clients over the last few years, we have developed some simple models that provide answers. I want to walk you through a step-by-step framework for designing digital shopper activity in Step 2. The key first step to making sense of these new, complex paths to purchase is to put the shopper's mission at the centre of a marketing plan is a good start. It's an approach that I call Mission Marketing.

Too Much Choice

There's an extremely entrenched idea in some sectors I work within that:

More consumer choice = More sales

The problem with this idea is a) it's not true and b) the principle leads to "shiny object syndrome" when it comes to using digital shopper marketing techniques as part of an integrated campaign.

One of the ideas driven by the rise of both supermarkets and brands was that consumers were looking for more choice. These days this concept manifests itself in "new news" and new product development. Brands will often allocate their largest budgets not to existing products that are proven sellers, but to NPD.

The NPD is used to make retailers excited and obtain more shelf space, when then brands will pay for media services space to get attention in store. You hear brand managers say: "Retailers like new news".

Well, is it any wonder when it's this new news and NPD that encourages brands to pay more money to retailers?

But does the shopper really benefit? In a famous experiment by Iyengar and Lepper from Columbia University and Stanford University, too much choice can be demotivating to shoppers and cause them to buy less.

As one of three experiments presented in their 2000 paper, "When Choice is Demotivating: Can One Desire Too Much of a Good Thing?", shoppers were given a choice of jams at a grocery store. One group of shoppers were shown six jams; another group, 24 jams.

The jams were showcased at a sampling station, and despite the different number of jams shown to the two groups of shoppers, there was little difference in their tasting behaviours.

The difference came in the buying behaviours. Thirty per cent of those shown only six jams went on to make a purchase. Of those shown 24 jams, only 3% bought something.

Iyengar and Lepper conclude by saying, "Even though consumers presumably shop at this particular store in part because of the large number of selections available, having 'too much' choice seems nonetheless to have hampered their later motivation to buy".

So choice is useful, but when the average large format supermarket stocks 35,000 to 45,000 different SKUs, the addition of every new product to your category could deliver diminishing returns and perhaps even reduce overall sales for your brand.

If you look at the rise of the High Street or local smaller supermarket store, one factor of their success is undoubtedly their localness and convenience for shoppers, but I wonder if part of that success is also down to the restricted numbered of SKUs on the shelf. Perhaps reduced choice (especially when you just need a few items to top up on during the week) actually increases basket spend by delivering ease of shop combined with attractive premium priced products.

But the concept of consumer choice being a good thing is a hard concept to shake, as it's so entrenched in our industry. But there is a way to solve this problem: using e-commerce. And it's an approach behind the impressive growth of Amazon.

Shiny Object Syndrome

One of the biggest problems clients have told me they've had over the last couple of years is keeping up with the pace of digital innovation. Many of our clients say that every week they have several calls from a variety of digital agencies, pure play specialists and technology companies that say they have the most exciting, newest digital innovation that will solve many of the client's problems.

These companies join the now-traditional digital companies offering web design and builds, SEO, social media marketing and email solutions. And because they are all saying that they are specialists, it leaves busy clients little time to stay fully up to date in all the areas of digital and to be able to properly evaluate the claims made by these companies.

For our friends at brands and retailers, often they are subject to shiny object syndrome, where the newest, the latest, the cleverest tech is presented to them as *the* answer. And many of our clients come to ask to help evaluate whether geo-located mobile ads, mobile footfall tracking or distributed e-commerce overlays are the right direction for them.

The people ringing from these companies and agencies are often wedded to their pure play approach or their single technological application, that they are no longer offering solutions based on what the brands and retailers need, but are only pushing what they sell. And next week, they'll be another agency or another technological innovation to sell. "Mobile? That was so last year. It's all about wearables now. Brand websites? Don't you have a curated content platform site yet?"

Of course, we both know that the "more is always better" approach is often wrong. The digital solutions are at best tactics, at worst another media or technology that seeks to fragment the path to purchase even further. The challenge is that many of these technologies will, over time, be driven by consumer uptake, so sooner or later brands and retailers may well need to consider them as part of their overall strategy.

But it's strategy that is the key word here. New technology and digital solutions should most often be considered within an overall integrated strategy to get the best results from it and to make sure that what you're buying really is fit for purpose to achieve your company's marketing and business objectives.

The funny thing is that, having worked as head of digital at an agency, you might expect me to be another voice pushing for the relentless increase of new technologies. But I spent at least a third of my time persuading brands and retailers that the digital solution they are considering is either wholly wrong in the light of their overall strategy, or its use and execution is a poor fit for their shoppers and consumers. My boss joked that when I'm in a room with potential new clients, he never knows if I'm going to get excited about the power of digital or start telling the prospects that cardboard POS will do a better job than whatever shiny object they are considering.

This pervasiveness and persuasiveness of shiny object syndrome was brought home to me recently when I spoke at an industry conference in London: IGD's Online & Digital Summit. I was asked to talk about mobile strategies for grocery retailers and supplier brands. This was made tricky by the fact that 80% of the speakers and sessions over the two-day event talked about the power of mobile and that this next year coming was going to be the year of mobile.

I think the organisers were expecting me to be another voice advocating the power of mobile, about how we had to talk to shoppers on their mobile devices, because, well, everyone has them.

Instead, the question I wanted to begin to answer was: Do we need a mobile app or not? It's an easier question to answer for grocery retailers than it is for supplier brands.

A 2014 survey by IGD shows that only 40% of UK shoppers say that have a useful grocery shopping app on their phone (compared with 72% who have useful online shopping apps in other categories), meaning there's lots of room for improvement – 60% of people have not found a reason to use grocery shopping apps. Using tablets and phablets to complete online grocery orders is increasing rapidly (while desktop use is declining), which means that there's a need to create apps that are easy to use and also very simple.

There's scope for someone to build an app that shoppers actually do love. Where's the app that makes the experience of online shopping – or shopper in-store assisted by an app – a pleasure? What's going to be the Uber or Hailo for shoppers?

Most large grocery retailers have an app, of course, so the simple answer: Yes, they should have an app. However, *what kind of app* is what grocery retailers need to decide on now. Most of the apps in existence turn shopping on an app just like shopping on a desktop, except with lots more scrolling.

The focus needs to be on ease of use first, then inspiration. How can you use my user data to give me a personalised app experience that curates the products I am most likely to want to buy? How can the app offer me relevant offers?

Two apps I've seen have a couple of great features that improves the shopping experience immensely. Morrisons' app allows you to create multiple shopping lists, which means I can have a list for a main shop, a list for occasional store cupboard essentials, a list for treats, etc. Allowing multiple lists makes scrolling through favourites and past shops for a handful of key items much easier.

Danish retailer Meny have the most beautiful looking grocery app I've seen. One page shows a simple screen that organizes recipes into sections such as meat, chicken, BBQ, street food, sweets, vegetarian, etc. When you click through to each recipe, the dishes have been shot like you'd expect in a glossy food magazine, and the ingredients are easy to add to basket. There's also a weekly meal planner that's easy to use, and to shop for however many members of your family you have. Meny makes shopping through an app inspiring and a pleasure.

What each country needs is at least one grocery app that has features and design like the examples mentioned above, as well as many others. Those grocers that develop these apps will not only win market share and lock in loyalty across online and physical stores, but also drive the use of online grocery shopping in general.

The question as to whether producers and brands should have their own app is a trickier one. Generally, the answer is: probably not. You have to ask yourself: "Do even loyal shoppers and consumers care enough about our brand to consider downloading an app, and even if they did, what can we do for them?"

There are exceptions, of course, where brands have such a deep connection to a territory or topic that it makes absolute sense to explore how an app in that area, brought to you by the brand, could add value to peoples' lives: Simple, who own the area of skincare, and more specifically sensitive skin; and Birds Eye/Iglo, who own the territory of family mealtimes, and whose mission statement is to: "To make better meals together. We create great tasting food to be enjoyed every day, at every meal, by everybody."

For every other brand, you have to consider that while enthusiastic brand managers might love the idea of having a little square logo on shoppers' and consumers' phones, do the shoppers care? Is it the right channel to use? Sure, you might set up an app for a specific game or content linked to a campaign, but once the interest in that content or game has died down, then what do you do with the app?

Perhaps you use the app to give shoppers a store finder, or for in-store navigation, or for mealtime inspiration, or for food matching? But is that what shoppers want – to consult a brand-specific app to solve those very narrow focused problems, when they are doing a shop that takes in many more grocery categories?

There's also an issue of regional coverage that's expensive to overcome. Some of the most valuable things a brand app could do are all in and around store.

You could, for example, use geo-located Push messaging to send people an offer within 500 metres of a store that stocks your products.

Or you could work with a retailer to place beacons in store so that when an app user entered the retailer, they'd receive a notification on their phone that provided an offer, inspiration or content to drive sales.

The ability for a supplier brand to use an app to drive store footfall or increase frequency of purchase or basket spend is very attractive, but the challenge is that unless you drive hundreds of thousands or millions of app downloads (which is expensive), you're not going to have a strong regional coverage or spread in any one location – say Manchester – which means that the geo-location campaign or the beacon campaign around Manchester stores will have a high cost per activation. Retailer apps, who already have millions of users, are much better placed to achieve their goals (and brand managers would be many times more efficient with their marketing spend by partnering with retail apps to trial these creative campaign ideas) than building their own app to achieve poorer results.

After briefly explaining this point of view to the 500 or so retailers and suppliers in the audience at the IGD digital conference, I got great feedback from those who came up to speak with me afterwards. "I'm so glad you told me to stay away from mobile apps," said one European brand manager. "My CMO has been asking me to look at mobile apps for ages, because mobile is the hot growth area, but I just didn't know what the right approach was."

While it might not necessarily be good business sense in the short term to advise clients to avoid from shiny object syndrome, I feel that in the long term it will be absolutely the right strategy. I'm not interested in here today, gone tomorrow technologies. I am interested in helping clients expand their digital knowledge and use when absolutely appropriate.

Just because something is *digital* doesn't mean that the age-old marketing planning rules don't apply. I always ask these questions when someone starts a conversation by mentioning a specific new technology or digital platform:

1. What's the business objective?
2. What are the marketing objectives?
3. What's the shopper and consumer insight?
4. What's the consumer behaviour?
5. What's the media landscape and channel usage for our shopper?
6. Does the implementation of these technologies smooth the path to purchase or introduce road bumps?

If you go through these steps when someone pitches you a new technology or digital use case, it's much easier to see the challenges and opportunities.

Of course, we don't always have time to go through that process every time someone approaches us with a new idea, which is why my number one goal with our clients is not to sell them more digital, but to be the number one trusted advisor when it comes to digital. The more I can help our clients navigate through the confusion and excitement that shiny object syndrome brings, the better the outcome for our clients, for their shoppers and consumers, and for us.

Zebra In A Supermarket

Imagine you walk into your usual grocery store to do a large shop. You're running through the list of items you want to buy in your head: tinned sweetcorn, pasta, oyster mushrooms, a stir-in sauce of some kind, and a posh dessert for Saturday…. And you turn down the next aisle, and there, in the middle of the aisle is a zebra.

There are tins and packets and boxes of food everywhere, knocked from the shelves. So much so that the floor a couple of metres around the zebra is almost impossible to walk on. Not that you're walking towards the zebra, because, well, there's a *zebra* in the supermarket!

The zebra looks up at you disinterestedly, and dips his head again to bury his mouth in a box of Cheerios. There are no clues as to how the zebra got there, there's no one else around to ask, and the mess in the aisles means that shopping in your usual way is impossible.

You stand there for some time watching the zebra eating away happily. Then you drop down your basket and go find a member of staff, wondering if they'll think you've gone mad when you tell them the news. Perhaps it's some kind of outlandish marketing stunt. Perhaps the zebra isn't really there and it's some clever projection or hologram. Perhaps you have lost touch with reality under the fluorescent lights of the store.

Whatever happens next, you're certainly not adding more items into your basket and the zebra is not exactly helping with ease of use of the store.

While personally I'd love to see zebras in supermarkets – hell, why not have a series of petting zoos? – that's not what I'm aiming to illustrate with this rather far-fetched anecdote.

The zebra in the story represents in-store technology.

Or rather, in store technology that's poorly conceived or poorly executed.

Here's one of the biggest challenges with emerging technology: If you execute cardboard point of sale materials poorly, at least people get what cardboard is and how it works.

You can look at it and think a freestanding display unit is ugly in its design, silly in the creative concept, placed in a strange or awkward location or is confusing in its message. But it's not as odd or disconcerting as a zebra in a supermarket aisle. You'll just ignore the bad POS, not trial or buy the product on promotion and move on with your existing planned shop, or continue to browse the shelves for inspiration elsewhere.

But if you conceive of bad digital ideas, or execute them poorly or inappropriately, it is like seeing a zebra in a supermarket – you stare at the strange new-fangled technology in store and wonder what on earth it is, what you're meant to do and how it works.

Except, unlike seeing a live zebra in an aisle, you'll not spend a long time watching him graze on Cheerios or admire his beautiful stripes. With bad tech, you'll probably feel discomfort that comes with confusion and that cognitive load of trying to assess the thing and figure out what to do will be too much and you'll just move on.

And that expensive digital trial someone thought would be amazing is now, like a zebra in a supermarket, an expensive headache. If you've ever encountered a QR code in store, been invited to use Blippar on a product or tried to redeem a mobile coupon on your phone, you too have seen a zebra in a supermarket.

I believe marketers should avoid the zebras and make technology fit for purpose, seamless, beautiful, ease to use and to add value to shoppers' lives in appropriate ways that build a deeper engagement with brands and retailers, and make you more sales.

So What Do Shoppers Want?

According to a survey of 1,000 UK shoppers by creative agency Live & Breathe, there are three areas that most shoppers think retailers and brands should focus their attention on in the coming years:

Cheaper prices – 53%
Better quality products – 44%
Better Customer Experience In Store – 34%

Elsewhere in the report, other key trends come through. One in five says that Click & Collect is the one technology that is changing how they shop the most. Parking, queues and noise also come under fire.

The shopper's message to us marketers is clear: focus on the basics of good products and good prices first, then give us an experience worth travelling for. If that includes appropriate use of digital, great.

Then make sure we can buy products when and where we like and pick them up from store later. It's a simple recipe that often gets over-complicated.

Key Points:
Overcoming Too Much Choice, Too Much Noise

- The path to purchase used to be simple: sofa to store. Now it's complicated as shoppers use the internet, e-commerce, social media and mobiles.

- Paths to purchase are no longer linear and the same for everyone. A shopper's path to purchase could be any combination of owned, earned and paid media in any and all channels, touchpoints and media.

- Understanding every shopper's path to purchase is impossible. Putting shopper missions at the centre of a marketing plan is a good start.

- Supplier brands and retailers have been told that never-increasing choice for the shopper drives sales. This is false. Too much choice reduces sales.

- Pure play agencies are pushing *the next big thing* in digital creating an atmosphere where marketers can succumb to Shiny Object Syndrome.

- When evaluating emerging technologies, consider the basics:

    1. Does this fit my larger business and marketing objectives?

    2. Does this suit my audience, shopper behaviour and insight?

    3. Does it *smooth the path to purchase* – add value or make things easier – or introduce technological "road bumps"?

- Bad digital executions are like seeing a zebra in a supermarket; you stare at the strange new-fangled technology in store and wonder what on earth it is, what you're meant to do and how it works. Our job is to keep the zebras out.

Jobs To Be Done:

- Understand your traditional and multi-channel paths to purchase for different shopper segments. Use an agency with strong shopper and/or retail insights.

- Speak with real shoppers to drill down into those paths to purchase further. Real insight often comes from real stories.

- Understand the ROI of investment into NPD and the effect on your offer as a whole. Is your rate of NPD growing the category or market share or is it consuming the shopper? Identify where budgets can be most efficiently spent for long-term returns.

Have a strategy to deal with the increasing number of digital technologies people want to pitch you. Perhaps work with an agency to help you focus only on what digital strategies are right for you, and deliver succinct updates and training to your team.

Step 1:

What is Digital Shopper Marketing? Defining The Role Of Digital

When I was told it was impractical to build an autonomous robot, I wanted to quit the after-school club. To my 12-year-old mind, a robot was an obvious choice. I could build the parts out of Technic Lego and create custom metal and wooden parts in the workshop.

The robot would always move forward when you set him on the floor, and use infrared sensors to adjust his course and avoid bumping into things. He'd have arms that could be remote controlled to pick things up. And he'd have light sensors that would activate lights, so (even though he had no eyes, besides the infrared proximity sensors), he'd give the impression of being able to see in the dark.

The technician of the after hours Design & Technology club was excited by my idea, but told me that it would just be too expensive to bring my robot to life. "All the technology you need is there or almost there to build it," he told me, "but the cost of the electronic components is beyond the budget we're suggesting to your parents."

Because I could imagine the robot moving on his caterpillar tracks, and turning as he approached a wall or a cat… because I had that movie in my head so clear… it took me a while to understand the practicalities that my teacher was bringing home to me. I like to think that a young Steve Jobs would have ignored the teacher and built a robot anyway.

My next idea was one I was sure was practical. I was learning in science classes that when you put acid in water, the number of available hydrogen ions increased. And because hydrogen ions are positively charged, that meant that you could detect the pH change using an electrode. Inside the electrode is pH7 water and when you dip the electrode in a more acidic solution, those positively charged hydrogen ions would cause a current to flow between the water and the solution you were testing.

I also learnt that as milk goes from fresh to off, there's a tipping point where the lactic acid in the milk increases. I wondered if you could build an electrode sensitive enough to monitor that pH change in milk and that an electrode dipped into your carton of milk in the fridge could easily tell you if the milk was about to go bad.

I imagined building an off milk sensor that would find its way into every home in the UK (my entrepreneurial vision didn't stretch to the world). No longer would anyone accidentally drink bad tasting milk or watch it curdle in their tea.

Excited, I took the idea to the after-school club technician. "Forget the robot," I said. "This idea will change the world." I remember the guy being impressed that I'd brought ideas from science class into Design & Technology (a discipline that only a year or two earlier had been called Woodwork, Metalwork & Plastics).

But then came the disappointment – or as I see it now, the reality check.

"Don't you think you're over-engineering this?" the technician asked. "Can't people just smell the milk? Plus, it will take a fair amount of tinkering to measure and alert people to such a small change in acidity of the milk."

Suddenly, my idea sounded silly. I'd over-thought the solution to a problem that really wasn't that big of a problem. Would people really make the time to remember to place an electrode in their milk in the fridge? Was I making the solution more cumbersome than the problem deserved?

The technician gave the 12-year-old my first lesson in copywriting for consumers. "Why don't the milk manufacturers just write 'Smell me before you pour' on the milk carton?"

I knew the technician had made a good point, but it took me a few days to accept it rather than just want to quit the club and not have to deal with him knocking my ideas. In the end, I designed a circuit that was a simple electronic keyboard. When you touched different keys on the circuit board, different notes would play. It was a simple project, but one that you could find in every *electronics for beginners* book.

Three years later I was in my final year of studying what was now called Craft, Design & Technology for GCSE. Forty per cent of the GCSE grade would come from a final year practical project of our own design.

We were told to design something that had a practical solution to a real-world problem. I found it difficult. When I did get an idea for the CDT project, it seemed boring at first.

We'd had a power cut at home, which were still not uncommon in the mid-80s. I remember my mum scrabbling in the dark for candles that were kept under the sink. The matches were kept in a high cupboard that Mum thought I didn't know about, as she'd hidden them after I had a phase of coming home from school and seeing what I could burn in the back garden.

A few days later, I asked Mum, "Why don't we have automatic lights that come on when it's dark?"

"I guess it's just too easy to turn on the light switch rather than build that into the electrics," she said.

"Okay, but was about when it's dark in a powercut?"

"That would be useful," she agreed.

"So why do homes have lights that come on in the dark in a powercut?"

"I guess no one's made one," she said.

That got me thinking. I was determined not to over-engineer to a problem this time. Powercuts happened often enough to be annoying. Perhaps not *that* annoying to most people, but what about for old people or disabled people? Or even kids like me who didn't know where the matches were kept? Why not make a light that would come on when there was a powercut and it was dark?

I took the idea to the CDT teacher.

"That's a really good idea, Vivian," he said. "Shall we sit down and talk about how to make it work?"

Over that discussion, we worked through the details. It would need to be small, so it could be conveniently placed at any point in a home, say the living room, or kitchen.

It would need a battery that would run a low-energy fluorescent tube, like the ones used in Exit signs in public buildings. And the battery would always need to be charged, so I found the perfect trickle charge battery that would be plugged into the mains socket. Next, I designed an electronic circuit that would trigger the fluorescent light when the power was cut and the light sensor said it was dark enough.

The project was easy enough to build and my dad helped me to show how simple it would be to fit into a home by building a life-size cross section of a floor and wall, complete with carpet, wallpaper and skirting board. The unit was housed in a box by the mains socket, and the light was housed higher up the wall in a separate box.

I got an A grade for Craft, Design & Technology.

While painful at the time, the lessons I learnt have stuck with me.

The robot was a great idea, but expensive. It would be hard to implement given my resources. This is exactly the same when planning digital ideas for shopping marketing briefs. While pure play digital agencies are able to go wild with digital executions that might work for an experiential event – it's a vending machine that when you smile at it, it cooks you fish fingers! – in the shopper environment, where cash is sunk on space and promotion in store, digital executions often can't cost an arm and a leg.

The bad milk sensor was over-engineered. You know those people who go on Dragon's Den or Shark Tank that's only an amazing idea to inventors? That was me. Sometimes a digital solution might sound cool and sexy, but the same problem might be solved more easily with print. It's a concept I use called *smoothing the path to purchase* that I'll talk about more in Step 2.

Being Right Now Is Better Than Being Right

Just a couple of years after I told my Design & Technology teacher about the robot with his amazing sensors, Lego released a number of components as part of its Technic range that would have made my robot a reality.

The constantly moving robot with an infrared obstacle detection isn't too dis-similar to something that's appearing in an increasing number of homes – the Roomba robot vacuum cleaner.

The milk sensor that tells you when your milk is going off… recently I saw some packaging innovation that had a colour-coded spot on a milk carton that told you how fresh your milk was.

Sometimes I like to imagine how rich and famous and successful I would be if I'd followed those ideas through.

But I'm reminded of a lesson from Steve Jobs and Apple: it's better to deliver things that are right for right now, rather than right at some indeterminate point in the future.

Steve Jobs was rarely first to a new category with Apple products. He was often slow to respond to a new field. Think of the iPod – there were digital music players for a few years before the first iPod was realized. The iPhone? Years late to the mobile phone market. The Apple Watch comes on the heels of dozens of quickly released smart watches and wearables.

What Apple does is attempt to come to a market that's ready for mass adoption. It releases 'new' products, designed beautifully into a market that's ready for everybody and their dog to buy one.

To be first with new technology is expensive and painful. As marketers of retail estates and FMCG brands, let's leave it to the luxury brands to trial new technology. The cost of being first on the high street or in the grocery store might be some extra PR, but it's also costly, confusing for the shopper, and it's more likely to fail with a mass-market audience.

Let's also not let our own level of digital knowledge – whether we're experts or near-luddites – affect our choice to trial technology. Let comparable case studies in other countries or other verticals influence us. Let consumer use of technology drive our decisions.

A Secret No-one Wants To Admit

Can I let you into a secret?

It's not really a secret.

It's something that we know as shoppers, but sometimes forget as marketers.

People don't buy stuff. They buy the feeling they get when they buy stuff.

If you buy new clothes or fish fingers, or a luxury yacht, what you're really buying is the good feeling you get. You want to feel smart or attractive or sexy or wanted or part of a club, or validated…. Or just that you've made a good choice for your family.

It's that feeling that drives your decision to buy or not to buy – and how much something is worth.

What if you're buying Tesco frozen peas because you always buy them? Surely you're just buying peas based on a basic need or a logical decision tree.

Well, yes, that's how it may look on the surface, but what you're also buying is the feeling of not having to think about the other frozen pea option, or whether to buy fresh peas, or a frozen green vegetable medley. You're buying certainty. The feeling of knowing what you like and the relief of not having to think about what to buy, and whether your decision is the best one for you or your family.

Neuroscience studies back this up. We don't make decisions by weighing up the evidence or examining hard facts, like many of us assume. Magnetic resonance imaging of the brain during the decision-making process shows that the amygdala lights up. The amygdala is deep in our old mammalian brain (much older than the cortex that handles rational thought) and its job is to attach feelings to events.

The amygdala lighting up when we have to choose between buying a Ferrari or a Saab is a godsend for us marketers: If you know what your customers care about, you can influence them to make a decision in your favour simply by giving them the feeling they want before they buy. And it's the same process at play when someone chooses a brand of fish fingers.

And here's the really cool thing: Because shoppers are buying this feeling in the first place, they are happy to be *influenced* to have more of this feeling.

Once you know the values and feelings that drive your shoppers to buy or not, you can use these to offer them your products and services in a way that will really resonate with them.

But there's one problem:

Most of us don't know precisely where our shoppers are or what they are doing most of the time – which makes it difficult to work out which channels we talk to them in, and how to connect these channels into a story that can increase the feelings people have when they walk into a store or go online.

Of course we know who our target shoppers and consumers are from our PEN portraits. But do we know how to deliver the following?

The right message
To the right person
At the right time
In the right context
In the right channel
With the right emotion
And the right level of personalisation?

It's the answers to the question above that is driving sales and brand loyalty for everything from fish finger brand, to preferred supermarket, to political vote.

And, of course, we know all this already, whether we think through the decision making process in this much detail, or just have a gut feeling that we need to appeal to something more than price and brand name.

The challenge of delivering effective marketing communications in a multi-channel world is huge. The pay off is big. Get it right and you can topple decades-old market leaders, or create a whole new market no one was expecting. Multi-channel marketing itself is a disruptive idea, using traditional and disruptive channels, so it's no wonder that digital is changing everything.

The aim of this book is to provide a snapshot in time to what's working now, and is an arrow that points in the direction of what we will mostly likely work in the future.

Whether your existing shoppers favour bricks or clicks, how we talk to them, about what, and when and whether we get a decent result no longer comes from the agency you hire or the brand equity. Instead, it comes from the level to which integrated multi-channel thinking can make shoppers feel great using messages and channels that naturally fit – and powerfully influence – their daily lives.

A Definition

Here's my personal definition of shopper marketing:

"All marketing activity developed based on a deep understanding of shopper behaviour, designed to engage the shopper and move him or her along the path to purchase."

Notice that last part: ...*along the path to purchase*. Shopper marketing is not only about the last mile to store and in store. It is marketing that thinks like a shopper or aims to flip the consumer into a shopper mind-set at all points towards purchase.

Sometimes I meet with people who haven't heard of shopper marketing at all, or they swap around the terms *shopper* and *consumer* indiscriminately. If you find yourself in similar conversations, here's an easy way to explain the difference:

Take dog food. The shopper is the pet owner, but you're not the consumer, right? Or, at least, not unless you're really hungry and have nothing else in the cupboards. In that case, we'd be crazy to market to the consumer, because they can't tell the shopper which brand to buy very well.

Now take beer. More men drink it but more women buy it during a big supermarket shop. In that case, we can influence the consumer with a TV ad or a print ad, but that doesn't make any difference if the shopper is a different person and decides to buy whatever is on offer in store.

You can use branding to help beer appeal to men, but along the path to purchase, we need to speak to women to choose our beer brand for their partner. That beer advertising is targeted (on the whole) towards men, when women more often buy it is one barrier towards a sale in store. Also, beer tends not to make it onto people's shopping list often, which can be another barrier to purchase.

Sometimes the shopper and the consumer are the same person – for example, when we pop into a shop to buy a snack. In that case, sometimes the consumer mind-set and the shopper mind-set are very different. The *consumer us* might been keen to eat our 5-a-day and usually brings apples to work to snack on. But the *shopper us* forgot to buy apples during the weekly online shop and now we're running late for a meeting and hungry.

We pop into a store and first area that we come across is the food to go section. They're offering crisps at a discount. And there's 20% more in them. We can't see where the apples are, but suspect they are further back into the shop. So the shopper quickly buys the crisps at the self-checkout machine. Whatever the best intentions were of the consumer us, the barrier was the available food to go selection, and the trigger was the promoted crisps and ease of shop.

Our job is to remove as many barriers to purchase as we can and use triggers to influence the behaviour of shoppers.

Feel free to adapt and steal the story as you see fit. If you work in non-FMCG retail, you can change the products to suit, based on your own market knowledge of shopper purchase behaviours.

Here's my definition of digital shopper marketing:

"Using technology on- and off-line to move people one or several steps along the path to purchase, and beyond."

What I'm saying is just like the way man uses a bicycle to make himself more effective, digital shopper marketing is using technology to leverage any shopper marketing efforts.

Notice that last part: *...along the path to purchase, and beyond.* The *beyond* part of the definition could be included in the shopper marketing definition too, but in the digital shopper marketing definition, it can have increased impact in helping people change their perceptions of the role of digital. *Beyond* is *at home* and *loyalty and advocacy*, areas where few digital marketers currently use digital from a shopper's perspective.

It means reminding shoppers to add store cupboard items to their online basket when it runs out. It means using email marketing and eCRM to drive shopper behaviour rather than purely thinking from a brand perspective. Shoppers are just as good advocates of a brand or product as consumers, and in many ways better.

Three Key Drivers

While digital shopper marketing is a relatively new area of focus, many of the principles behind it are driven by the same principles as 'traditional' shopper marketing. These are the key three business drivers of digital shopper marketing:

1. Media dilution

The vast increase in the number of media channels drove the need to no longer rely on broadcast media to talk to shoppers. In the digital world, every shopper can make a YouTube video and influence another; every blogger and every comment on social media can affect a shopping decision, for good or bad.

Gaining cut-through and reach is declining in traditional media. Stores can be seen as a large mass media channel to communicate in. But attention is fragmented there too. Digital offers cut through along the path to purchase, in store and beyond to gain both mass attention and personalised individual attention of target shoppers.

2. Shopper behaviour

A number often quoted by shopper marketers is that 50% of final brand and pack choice is made in store. The truth is that that figure varies widely depending on which study or survey you take notice of. The key point is that retail and brand loyalty are much harder to obtain for long periods of time as 30 years ago.

Many shoppers in the grocery market are brand switchers. Many High Street retailers have suffered due to the rise of online shopping. The value of digital shopper marketing is to use digital touchpoints, media and touchpoints to increase the number, frequency or effectiveness of marketing messages to better engage with shoppers and to build loyalty in the channels that shoppers are paying attention in.

3. Influence of retailers

Compare today's retail stores to those of 50 years ago. They are much more sophisticated and complex now. Complexity can lead to confusion and reduce shopper interaction. In grocery, retailers control the look and feel of supplier brand messages, their number and positioning. The relationship with the shopper is with the retailer. Digital shopper marketing allows the brands to shift the needle back in favour of the brands, but owning more of the bath to purchase with digital messaging.

For retailers, the tension between High Street sales, out-of-town retail parks and e-commerce sales has made a multi-channel offering a necessity. To avoid your brick and mortar shopper using your competitor to do their online shopping, you must offer them an online experience as seamless and valuable as the in-store one.

These three key drivers mean that I advise clients to align their shopper marketing strategies within their marketing mix so that they have a *shopper back approach*.

This doesn't mean that shoppers are more important than consumers, or that brand marketing or ATL channels are not valued, but rather that the object of much of that marketing is to influence a sale. And that whether the shopper is a different person or the same person as the consumer, their mind-set when making purchasing decisions is what should be considered first to ensure that all marketing efforts align to help weight that decision in our favour.

4. The power of mobile

Supplier brand sand retailers may try to control the channels and media where consumers and shopper interact with them, but the ubiquity of mobile devices means that personal computing becomes a key factor in those interactions. Tablets are becoming a key device for online research and shopping. Mobiles will become the default digital space for interacting with brands in store (rather than clunky screens). Wearables have the potential to personalize and miniaturise interactions with retailers and brands, driving the need for personalised and efficient messaging.

Consumers Vs. Shoppers

Everyone has a film that has affected him or her in some way. Whether your favourite movies are ones that make you laugh, keep you on the edge of your seat, thrill you, scare you, make you sad, or move you in some other way, we've all been moved by films.

When you think about what is going on for a moment, it's a bit weird. We sit in a movie theatre or at home in front of the TV and some pixels on a screen change colour alongside an audio track. What we're watching is entirely made up. It's not real. Yet, when we're on the edge of our seats, crying with laughter or tears or are scared, the emotions we're experiencing feel very real.

To our minds and bodies, what we're experiencing might as well be reality. Numerous scientific studies have shown that our minds treat imagined experiences as if they are real. A study that looked at which neurons fired when footballers kicked a football during a match, found that supporters also had the same areas of the brain light up when they watched. They were imagining kicking the ball too, and to their mind there was no difference between actually kicking the ball and just imagining it.

Similar studies were done with piano players and piano players who only imagined playing. The same areas of the sensory cortex lit up with both activities. In many ways, our shoppers and consumers are like those football players and piano players in the studies. The same person may at one time be a shopper and at another time be a consumer. What's important is what's going on in their mind when we talk to them.

They may be at home flicking through posts on Facebook eating their fish fingers for dinner. They may be in consumer mode. But we can post an advert on Facebook that makes them consider being in the shopper mind-set. And thinking about being a shopper will light up same or similar areas of the brain as actually doing the shopping. This is why we always need to consider not whether people are shoppers or consumers, but which mind-set they are in.

A consumer's mind-set
What goes through their mind when deciding what product to use?

A shopper's mind-set
What goes through their mind when deciding what product to choose?

Currently, many marketing and sales channels almost exclusively focus on delivering content and messaging that is either specific to the consumer's mind-set or the shopper's mind-set.

For example, many brands use social media to talk to consumers. A fish finger brand might create a Facebook post that says:

"Click Like if you're having fish fingers for dinner!"

Clearly, this message is focused on the consumer.

But what if we wanted to talk to the shopper? How might we write a post on Facebook? Perhaps something like this:

"Have you tried these new fish fingers yet?"

Because the post emphasizes trial, which requires purchase, we're speaking to the reader in a shopper's mind-set.

In this example, the consumer and the shopper might be different people, such as a man who has bought the weekly shop and is cooking fish fingers for his wife for dinner.

Or the consumer and the shopper could be the same person, and at home they are in a consumer mind-set while in the store they are in a shopper's mindset.*

While social media is often a channel used by brands to talk to the consumer, in this case we can effectively talk to viewers of the Facebook post and aim to shift their mind-set into a shoppers' mind-set (if it isn't currently).

By only talking in a consumer's mind-set we miss out on the ability to affect people who are about to move another step along the path to purchase.

If we include social media posts designed to move people into a shopper's mind-set, we'll reach a segment of viewers who are entering the path to purchase at a point when we can begin to influence their purchase and put those new fish fingers on the shopping list for consideration.

This is why shopper marketing is most effective when we use it to influence shopper behaviour during a shopping trip, and before and after those trips. Because being a shopper is a mind-set as well as an activity, we want to effectively talk to that shopper mind-set at appropriate points throughout the consumer/shopper lifecycle.

*(Actually, it's not quite that simple, a point which basic consumer/shopper marketing explanations overlook. Fred might be the shopper. At home, Fred's girlfriend Jenny might be the cook. Fred and Jenny might be both eating fish fingers for dinner. So who is the consumer here: the cook or the people sitting down to eat? The answer, of course, is both. But the key question is, if you wanted to influence future shopper behaviour that started in the shopper environment, where is your best leverage point: the shopper, the cook, or one or other of the diners?)

Five Hats

"The customer is always right" may be a good maxim to life your work life by if you only have one customer. The challenge for us marketers is there is always more than one customer who at times needs to be treated like a king.

Owner managers of Mom and Pop stores (i.e. those who are not so au fait with large estates, shareholders, suppliers, and shopper marketing principles) usually only have to wear one hat and one pair of shoes – those of the customer.

Those of us in retail marketing of larger estates (especially those whose company is publically traded on the stock market) know that there is always more than one customer who we need to treat as king:

- The shareholders

Those of us working for a manufacturer or supplier brand have these customers to treat as king:

- The shopper
- The consumer
- The shareholders
- The customer (i.e. the retailer)

As a marketing agency that specializes in retail and activation through the lens of the shopper mind-set, we have these customers we need to treat as king:

- The client (hello you!)
- The shopper
- The consumer
- The shareholders
- The customer (i.e. the retailer)

Often the briefs we get from clients brush over or ignore the inherent conflict between having so many kings to make happy. The supposedly single-minded approach to change the behaviour of the shopper just got a lot more complex than it was on paper.

Another common issue is an FMCG supplier brand proposing a campaign to influence shopper behaviour, but their approach and output of that campaign in store is driven in large part due to what the retailer will allow the supplier brand to get away with.

Imagine a retailer saying that all freestanding display units must adhere exactly to the retailer guidelines in build, look and feel. While wearing the retailer hat, we can see the retailer's point of view, as they want to maintain a consistency of brand and an ease of shop. While wearing the supplier hat, they of course want their FSDU to stand out and to be disruptive in the aisle. In effect, their ideal scenario is the opposite end of the spectrum to the retailer.

Some agencies will explain to the client that the retailer guidelines must be followed almost entirely, in which case they've made the retailer king and ignored the needs of their client, the supplier brand. Other agencies will initially ignore retailer guidelines and design something totally brand led, and nine times out of ten the retailer will reject the FSDU and they won't get it away at all.

This is why I believe the shopper must be king. When we put the shopper front and centre, we can use best-in-class executions backed up by shopper insight and sales figures to deliver a rationale and an argument that informs just how much influence brand and retailer and shopper should have in what that FSDU looks like.

Take this gondola end for Peroni.

Consider it wearing the hat of the retailer and it doesn't make sense: it doesn't look like any other gondola end and it breaks all the rules of product density on the shelves.

But wear the hat of the shopper and the rational becomes clear.

Beer is often forgotten from shopping lists.

Men drink more beer; women do more large shops.

When beer drinkers come home and the beer is in the cupboard, it's annoying.

The solution? Sell beer cold in store to remind the shopper that the consumer likes to come home to cold beer. Could it be that if beer is merchandised chilled, then it reminds the shopper about cold beer, so they buy more of it… and then they put that beer straight in the fridge when they get home?

Why not create a gondola end that:

- Looks stunning and premium (the brand is king)
- Uses shopper insight (the shopper is king)
- Puts cold beer in the fridge at home more often (the consumer is king)
- Acts as a beacon in the beers, wines and spirits category and uplifts sales (the retailer is king)
- Shows innovation in technology and drives sales, adding to the argument that Tesco is leading the way and adding to the company value (the shareholder is king)

If we drop the hat metaphor for now and couch what we're saying in more marketing language, we think the best way to reduce conflicts is to map out in advance:

What are the retailer objectives?
(Business objectives; marketing objectives; positioning; press scrutiny; corporate social responsibility)

What are the supplier brand objectives?
(Business objectives; marketing objectives; positioning; press scrutiny; corporate social responsibility)

What are the shopper objectives?
(Triggers; barriers, both conscious and unconscious. How do we deliver the right message, at the right time, to the right person, in the right channel or medium?)

What are the consumer objectives?
(Consumer insight; consumer behaviour; influence and leverage with shopper)

The reality might sometimes be that we cannot remove all conflicts between these different objectives, but the goal of a shopper-centric approach is that 1) we put the shopper first and 2) shopper insight can be used to align all the other parties.

When we get it right, we get a win-win-win-win for retailer, supplier brand, shopper and consumer... which means that we as an agency win too.

Smoothing The Path

Have you used Uber, the taxi-booking app? It's really good at making life so much easier for the shopper.

Once you've downloaded the Uber app, hailing a cab is much easier than standing on the street waiting for one to arrive, or using a taxi phone number. You open up the app and can see in real time your location and the location of the nearest available taxis. You tap in the postcode of where you want to go, a taxi is assigned to you and you can see its progress as it comes to collect you. You can see how much the fare will be, and you can pay automatically via the linked bank account or PayPal account in the app, eliminating the need for cash.

Uber is a near-perfect examples of what I call *smoothing the path to purchase*. And it's this aspect of digital shopper marketing that is one of the most powerful tools in my box.

With digital shopper marketing, we still need to wear the hats of the retailer, supplier, shopper and consumer, of course. The challenge with technology is that all too often, when poorly executed, it does not meet the shopper's objective, but instead opposes it.

For a couple of months I became obsessed with Jimmy's Iced Coffee. Every morning on my way to work, I'd visit the WH Smiths at Brighton train station and buy one. And every morning for those two months, I'd see the newly launched Juice Burst on the shelves of the drinks chiller as I picked up my Jimmy's.

The graphic on the Juice Burst pack was of exploding fruit, and right beneath was a Blippar logo. Perhaps you've come across Blippar; perhaps you've Blipped yourself, perhaps not. Blippar is an augmented reality app. Using it, brands can allow users to see digital animations float over the top of the product or advert it's used with.

Right below the Juice Burst bottles on the shelf was a barker with a price promotion I no longer remember. On the barker was another call to action to use Blippar on the bottle, saying something like *watch the fruit explode*.

Now here's the problem. I'm at the train station. Which means I'm either in a hurry, or have time to kill. Mobile reception is okay, but not great. And most people do not already have Blippar on their phone. The barker is aiming to get across both a price promotion to drive trial of the new drink, and to drive a digital activation of the drink in the hope that the engagement is disruptive enough so that it drives further trial, or at least a talking point among friends and colleagues. That's a hell of a lot of information to get across in a barker when a glance in store is less than half a second.

Let's say I do see the Blippar logo. Do I even understand what it is? Even if there is a clear call to action to download the app from the Apple store or Google Play store, so I have the mobile reception, the data allowance, and most importantly the time and inclination to do so… it's a drink. With exploding fruit. What's the *what's in it for me?* to take these steps? Is this really going to entertain me more than spending my time and data on watching funny YouTube clips?

Let's say I do download the app and wait. Then I have to Blip the product – the app opens the camera and the app recognises the object in front of it to deliver the right animation. This process is not seamless at the moment. It takes a couple of seconds. Finally the animation of an exploding bottle is shown. It's quite nice, but it's not thrilling, hilarious or wildly entertaining. My 14-year-old niece would give it a "Meh!" before switching back to WhatsApp or YouTube.

After the animation plays out, there were options to take further actions, like go to the website (but without a strong *what's in it for me?*).

If I'm in a hurry, am I really going to do all this? Even if you have time to kill waiting for my next train, would you do this?

There are two problems with the Juice Burst Blippar activation. One is that the technology used does not smooth the path to purchase. The other is thinking about the interaction from a brand + consumer perspective instead of a shopper perspective.

The point of smoothing the path to purchase is to remove any road bumps – or blocks – between what the shopper intends to do and what we ideally want the shopper to do. The shopper in this case was looking for a drink. If you use technology, or POS, or any method – disruptive, innovative or traditional – to help sway my decision towards buying a different drink instead, you want to make that transition as smooth as possible. If you opt for solutions that introduce road bumps to choose your product, I'm going to probably choose my existing path to purchase.

Of course, things aren't really this clear cut. There are three considerations when working with the *smoothing the path to purchase* concept:
1. All advertising and marketing are in some form a road bump. Whether that's a shelf barker that demands my attention and – momentarily – interrupts my path to purchase, or an online ad that calls for attention when I'm chatting with friends on Facebook, there's always small road bumps. Our job is to make them as small or non-existent as possible.

2. Shoppers bring their own road bumps with them, or in traditional shopper marketing terms, *barriers*. I might not know what I want to drink. That cognitive load of indecision or confusion is a road bump. I might not be sure if I have enough cash and am unsure if cards are accepted.

Our job as marketers is to take the opportunity to smooth out the road bumps the shopper brings to the path to purchase. Confused? Let us show you a barker, or a neck collar, or a digital shelf strip that helps you decide in our favour. Are your online shopping delivery charges expensive? Let us pay for them for you, or make them seem less expensive, so you can get on with your shopping.

3. The technology you use may not be clear and simple to everyone. Even taking a phone out of your pocket is a road bump. But we can focus on making the *what's in it for me?* so great that the road bumps is small by comparison. The bigger the benefit to the shopper to take our preferred path to purchase, the bigger the road bump can be and still deliver the result we want.

Imagine if that Blippar was to win a multi-million pound mansion every day for a month, plus a sports car and a speedboat, plus paid-for holidays for life – you might be more inclined to Blip. Digital activations can deliver value that overcomes road bumps with a great offer, a value add, by making shopping easier or making them more engaging.

If you want me to download a mobile app that will take my shopping list and quickly guide me around store to where the items are, then the value of saving time might well overcome the road bump of using the app for the first time. If you show me content on a screen in store that makes the retail experience much more pleasant, engaging or entertaining, then the value of that content will most likely overcome the minor road bump of stopping in front of the screen that demands my attention.

The net affect of smoothing the path to purchase using digital is to have less road bumps than the value the shopper receives.

All digital shopper-marketing activations should have the goal of smoothing the path to purchase. Remember, my definition is digital shopper marketing:

"Using technology on- and off-line to move people one or several steps along the path to purchase, and beyond."

People will move forward more easily when we smooth the path. Like our man with a bicycle, the technology should enable both marketers and shoppers to achieve their missions more quickly.

Five Hats, Five Promises

Remember our five hats?

- The client
- The shopper
- The consumer
- The shareholders
- The customer of FMCG brands (the retailer)

We can use the definition of digital shopper marketing and some of the principles discussed to develop some promises to our five hat wearers.

My Promise To Clients

I will use technology throughout the shopper journey to:

1. Engage people emotionally, increasing brand equity, by delivering the right message to the right person in the right location at the right time. Communications to the shopper and consumer are at scale, while also targeted, segmented and personalised where appropriate, to help the shopper make a better decision (in favour of our client).

2. Smooth the path to purchase, increasing footfall, volume sales and average transaction value and basket spend, as appropriate, while satisfying brand, customer and consumer objectives too.

3. Increase customer lifetime value through loyalty and advocacy by adding value to the shopper (whether that's savings, emotional satisfaction, meaningful engagement, help or information)

Shopper Promise:
We will use technology to make shopping better: whether that's making shopping easier, better value, more fun, satisfying, or helping you make your shopping decisions more easily.

Consumer Promise:
We will use technology to help you get more from what you buy: Whether that's making cooking easier and eating more fun, making your purchases more valuable, useful, fun, satisfying and engaging, making it easier for you to buy more of what you like, or making it easier for you to talk with other consumers and shoppers and to brands and retailers.

Promise To Shareholders (both my employer and my clients):
We will partner with you to use technology throughout the shopper journey to:

1. Smooth the path to purchase, increasing footfall, volume sales and average transaction value and basket spend, as appropriate.

2. Provide you with digital thought leadership to make more efficient and effective use of technology.

Step 1 Key Points:
What is Digital Shopper Marketing? Defining the role of digital

- People don't buy stuff. They buy the feeling they get when they buy stuff. Digital activations need to stimulate that feeling before shoppers buy.

- A digital shopper marketing definition: *Using technology on- and off-line to move people one or several steps along the path to purchase, and beyond.*

- Four key drivers make digital shopper marketing necessary: media dilution; changing shopper behaviour; the power of the retailer; the power of mobile.

- Talk to a shopper's mind-set: "Click Like if you're having fish fingers for dinner" focuses on the consumer. "Have you tried these new fish fingers yet?" speaks to someone in a shopper's mind-set, and encourages them to think *shopper* even if they are in a consumer mind-set.

- There are up to five people to consider with digital strategy: the shopper, the consumer, the shareholders, the supplier's customer, or the retailer's supplier.

- Use technology to smooth the path to purchase, to remove any road bumps between what the shopper intends to do and what we want the shopper to do.

Jobs To Be Done:

- Pick a core audience segment. Discuss: What feeling did they have after purchasing? How is their day/life different before and after purchase?

- Identify the key drivers that are making digital shopper marketing more important in your industry and job. Is it above the line media fragmentation, changing shopper behaviour, the power of mobile, or something else?

- Write two example Facebook posts for your brand. One that focuses on the consumer e.g. "Click Like if you're having fish fingers for dinner." Write another that speaks to someone in a shopper's mind-set, and encourages him or her to think *shopper* even if they are in a consumer mind-set – e.g. "Have you tried these new fish fingers yet?" Discuss with your copywriters and agency.

- Choose a recent integrated campaign or marketing activity and identify that hats you had to wear to get the work away. Identify the objectives that each hat wearer had, and the influence on the final output – did one hat wearer start off as more important, but another set of objectives became key in the final execution? Check that you have an agency in place that puts the shopper first.

- Use my promises to develop your own guarantees for how you and your team use digital in your marketing. The promise to: the shopper, the consumer, the shareholders, any other parties. Ask yourself, "'Is the shopper king?' in my written promises."

Step 2:

Owning The Path To Purchase

Here's the problem:

No one knows what they're doing.

No one knows the answer to the question: What's the best way to market stuff in a multi-channel digital world?

The brave (and the most honest) hold our hands up and say "We're really not sure how all this stuff – smartphones, smart TV, beacons, in-store tech, social media, beacons, email marketing and web – all works together.

The rest of us are making it up as we go along, learning along the way.

The trick is to understand enough about the shopper barriers and triggers, the audience and capabilities of channels and tech and to piece together a hypothesis that can be tested and refined, tested and refined.

Digital – and integrated marketing – requires an obsession to detail, a desire to join things up, and an ability to stick to a feedback loop: test, learn, tweak… and test again.

Digital is confused and confusing to many of us because there are three key issues getting in the way of the simple approach that digital and truly integrated marketing now requires:

1. Many of us think in terms of campaigns instead of 'always on' digital activations.

That means that by the time we're able to talk to enough people along the path to purchase and learn what's working and what isn't, it's time to move on to another campaign, with the learnings often never captured.

It's like learning to ride a bike, and just as the stabilisers come off, we decide to ride the unicycle. The moment we're in on the unicycle, we decide to learn to horse ride. And then we pretend to be experts in all 3 disciplines when we've only learnt the basics.

2. People say, "But you can't properly measure digital, can you?"

To which the answer is, "Yes there are still some issues about fully joined up single consumer view tracking, but it's a lot more trackable that traditional marketing ever was."

The challenge is that measurability is an easy stick to beat digital with, and often an excuse to not move forward with digital trials. But how robust are your numbers on tracking the eyeballs on your print campaigns, your in-store POS, or how those TV views convert at each stage along the path to purchase?

Digital doesn't have all the answers, but it's also not the biggest problem or the biggest block in increasing ROI efficiency of shopper campaigns.

3. We're not joining this stuff up enough.

The path to purchase is no longer a linear one. The golden days of someone watching a TV ad then going in store to buy our product has been replaced by a looping, forked, convergent and divergent ball of string.

Like one of those maze puzzles in colouring books we had as children, on the left-hand side is one end of the piece of string (the start of a shopper journey) then there is a huge, looping, messy maze, and on the right is the other end of the string (the sale). And in between are all the traditional and newer channels, touchpoints and media from which shopper and consumers jump between.

Whatever we think our campaigns should do, our shoppers and consumers are probably doing something different, and in order to maximize our reach and our ability to move people along the path to purchase with success and efficiency, we need to be joined up inside our organisations.

Brand teams need to talk to shopper teams, who need to talk to retail teams, who need to talk to e-commerce teams, who need to talk to experiential and PR, to digital and sales promotion teams. All too often one department doesn't communicate to another. It's siloed off, with each department trying to solve the same maze while only looking at one small section.

These three big problems are those that our shoppers and consumers don't care about or notice. They only buy or don't buy. They either trial or don't trial. They either develop a relationship with a brand they like, or they don't.

So what's the answer to making sense of a multi-channel and digital world?

Part of the answer is to understand the changing technology landscape. It's also about going back to basic shopper marketing principles and applying them to new technologies.

Traditional Linear View

While all marketing models are flawed – a best-fit approximation of what we'd hope ideal consumers and shopper would do – some models are flawed more than others. And the most flawed model is one that attempts to suggest that the path to purchase is a linear one.

Exhibit A – Take a look at this typical linear model:

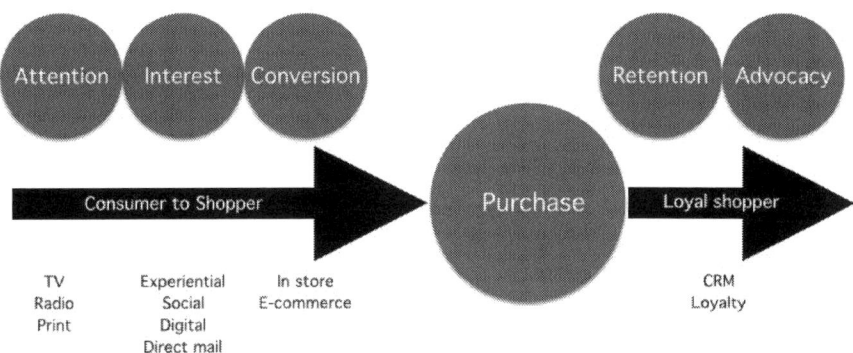

It suggests that someone starts life as a prospect until we drive awareness with above-the-line media, then they are taken to a second step where we use digital, experiential, social or direct marketing to interest (or engage with) the prospect.

Next, we meet them in store or in an e-commerce store where they can be converted into purchasing. After purchase, we can retain them using a loyalty scheme or communications in CRM channels.

If only life was that easy!

As consumers and shoppers ourselves, we can easily pick apart this model and find its flaws. People do not necessarily move from the Awareness phase to Interaction to Conversion to Purchase and Retention.

They may stay in one phase forever and never move forward. They may move from seeing a TV ad to a social media site, then see several more TV ads before buying. They may buy, then be made aware of the above-the-line activity much later. Or they may be made aware through a friend, or a social media post, or ad, instead of traditional ATL activity.

This model also assumes that people all have a consumer mind-set when presented with ATL and a shopper mind-set as they encounter BTL activity. Again, this is not necessarily true. You could be watching TV while filling in your online shopping order on your iPad and be very much in the shopper mind-set while the TV ads play.

Equally, you can be in store and have no intention to buy. Your husband might have dragged you to a shop with him, and you're starving and can't wait to get out to go to Pret A Manger and grab lunch. Your environment might be a grocery store, but your mind-set might be as a consumer.

Some Alternative Models

The truth is that the path to purchase looks a lot more like this:

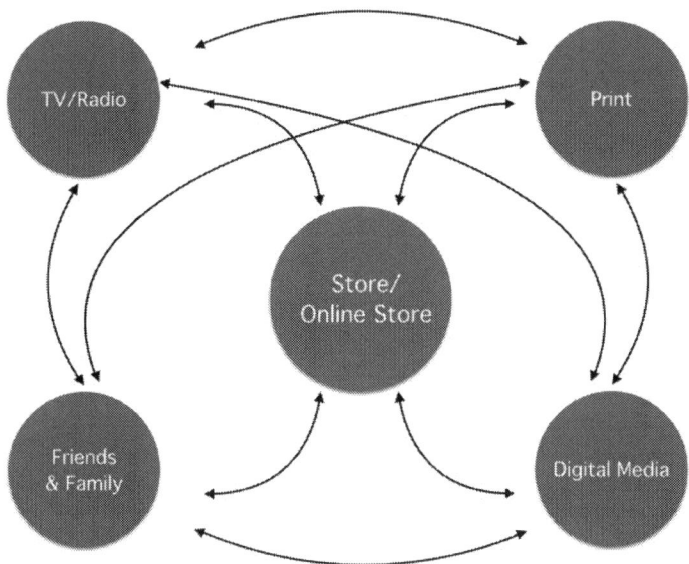

In this model, online and physical stores have been placed at the centre, with TV, radio, print and digital media and friends and family recommendations all feeding in to drive sales. But the online store and physical stores also act as a mass communication media channels and also drive consumers and shoppers to all other nodes of the model.

While this model looks pretty because all nodes interact with all others, it tends to suggest that all channels have equal effect on shopper and consumer behaviour and does not take into account of shopper and consumer mind-sets.

This model is interesting:

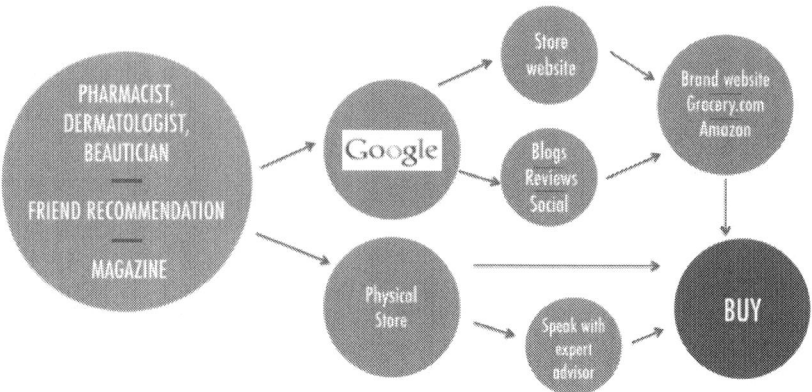

Taken from some work I carried out for a skincare brand, this model is more specific than the others. By focusing on a specific category, or group of products, this model allows you to use data and insight to map out a path of purchase that is closer to what shoppers are actually doing.

This model involves friend and professional recommendation, plus the role of using digital to research online, before either doing nothing, purchasing online, or purchasing in a brick and mortar store. It also recognises the role of blogs, rating and reviews and social media along the path to purchase.

The downside of course is that shoppers might not always be moving from left to right in a simple linear way. They might be moving two steps forward, then one step back, for example, on a friend recommendation, Googling a brand and going to a brand website, only to go back to Google for a better answer.

The shopper might also be creating much more complicated and lengthy paths to purchase (or indeed paths to non-purchase). On a friend recommendation, the person might Google a brand and visit a brand website, then decide to take a look in a Boots when they are next in town.

Armed with new knowledge, they might go home and read a bunch of reviews on Mumsnet, or another forum, then download a skincare app, Like a couple of Facebook pages and loiter for several months before visiting Amazon to buy a product.

A better model can only overcome some of the limitations I've pointed out above. As I said, all models are flawed. And no model can make sense of the complexity of the path to purchase in the age of digital, nor can it account for every consumer's and shopper's different paths to purchase.

That's why I like to think of the model I use with my clients as more of a system, or way of thinking – a starting point of how to consider the consumer and shopper in a complicated world – rather than a definitive answer.

A New Model: The Consumer-Shopper-Consumer Lifecycle

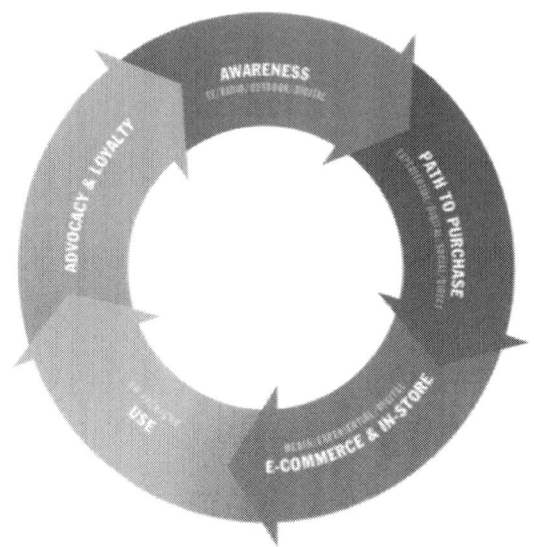

When I talk through this model to clients, I start at the top of the circle with the Awareness phase. This could also been considered where traditional above-the-line channels sit. But digital also sits here. The key idea is that awareness can come from any marketing communication, and also recognising that these days, digital channels can have wide reach in the same ways as does TV, print and out-of-home communications.

This model is an attempt to place all digital channels and technologies in the context of the entire consumer to shopper to consumer lifecycle. It puts the shopper mind-set at the heart of our thinking alongside the consumer mind-set – and rather than separating out different elements of the path to purchase, this model recognises the path to purchase as an important phase in the consumer-shopper lifecycle, but also recognises other (often overlooked) phases as equally important.

The Consumer-Shopper-Consumer Lifecycle: Awareness

In the Awareness phase, many people will be in the consumer mind-set, but some will already be in a shopper mind-set and ready to buy. (Think of someone browsing Tesco.com making a groceries order and seeing a banner ad for a relevant product. That might be the first time they are made aware of the product or promotion or new campaign, and they are already in shopper mode.) This model recognises that there are consumers and shoppers in a varying mix, all the way from the Awareness phase through to purchase in-store or an E-commerce store.

However a consumer or shopper is made aware of the product or retailer, they then progress to the Path to Purchase. In this phase, key channels are often – but not always – experiential, digital, social, direct ad…

The Consumer-Shopper-Consumer Lifecycle: The Path To Purchase

The path to purchase as we said before might be simple and linear, or it could be looping and convoluted with steps forwards and backwards and steps repeated as media reinforces the brand, shopper value, consumer value, promotion or campaign through repetition and recognition. The person may move back and forth between a consumer and a shopper mind-set throughout this phase. They may progress towards a purchase, or they may never purchase, or they may purchase a competitor product or from an alternative retailer.

The Consumer-Shopper-Consumer Lifecycle: E-commerce & In-Store

In-store and e-commerce is the next phase where the individual enters a store in a consumer or shopper mind-set (perhaps depending on whether they have chosen to go to the store or be invited along by a partner, relative or friend). In e-commerce, the person could have arrived at a transactional site, but still only be researching the product and flip between a consumer mind-set and consideration for the product and a shopper mind-set.

An example of this is buying a car with your partner. To be a little bit sexist for a moment, to make a clear point, I may want a sports car and my partner might want a people carrier for the family. Which car we want to use and drive around in is all about the consumer mind-set.
However, if I say I want a sports car, my partner might say it's too much money to spend. She counteracts my consumer mind-set with a shopper perspective. She might then talk about how practical it would be to have a car that can fit in two kids' car seats, a boot full of shopping and still have room to put the kids' bikes on the roof. I could counteract her consumer mind-set by saying that a competing model is on promotion, and would save us a lot of money, but it doesn't have the roof rack.

The Consumer-Shopper-Consumer Lifecycle: Consumer Use

The next phase is the most under-utilised by shopper and retailer marketers – or marketers in general: Use. This is the period of time after the person, who is in the shopper mind-set, has made the purchase and is now using it, or consuming it, whether that's at home, at work or on the go.

Because shopper marketing has traditionally focused on getting people to the point of purchase, then making a decision in the favour of the product, we seem to have forgotten the very reason the person is buying the product: because it has value.

If I buy fish fingers in a Morrisons store, there is probably a period of time while I am in the store where my mind-set shifts between that of a shopper and that of a consumer and back again, before I make a purchase.

Consumer: I must remember to buy fish fingers, because Jasper said he wanted them for dinner tonight.

Shopper: Oh look, this brand is on deal.

Consumer: Birds Eye fish fingers do taste great, and I want to make sure Jasper eats the ones he loves.
Shopper: I could save £1 if I buy that other brand, though.

And so on…

Once the person in store has shifted between a shopper's consideration and a consumer's consideration and makes the purchase, what that person does next is largely ignored by marketers – which is strange when you consider that what happens next is often key to their future purchase consideration.

Imagine I'm now at home making Jasper fish fingers for dinner. There are some key factors and events that will affect the future relationship with the brand: my ease of cook, how much Jasper (and I) like eating them, and what I do or think next about the brand in relation to my next shop.

This Use phase of a product is perhaps mostly the domain of the consumer's mind-set. And that makes it a great, untapped opportunity for marketers. Imagine your ideal prospect having a great experience of using or consuming your products. Imagine now that you use a print or digital activation on the packaging to develop a deeper relationship with the brand, and then shift them into a shopper's mind-set with a suggestion or call to action around future purchases…

The Consumer-Shopper-Consumer Lifecycle: Loyalty & Advocacy

To many shopper marketers, this phase usually doesn't sit under their remit either. Advocacy is seen as a series of activity driven by brand; loyalty is often looked after by a loyalty team, focusing on loyalty cards, or perhaps a digital team using E-CRM channels.

I think that keeping this key area of the consumer-shopper-consumer lifecycle siloed off like this is a mistake. Loyalty cards (and more recently app-based and web-based loyalty schemes) are all about the smart use of data. E-CRM is the integrated of digital channels such as social, mobile, email and web, alongside more traditional channels such as direct mail to build deeper and longer relationships with shopper and consumers.

Loyalty and advocacy can be much better leveraged to shift thinking from *consumer* and *brand* to also include consideration in the shopper mind-set. Most emails sent out by FMCG brands tend to focus on the relationship between consumer and brand. What we explore in Step 5 is the value of deliberately developing strategy and the marketing communications that talk to the end user in the shopper mind-set to drive future purchases.

We also look at how we can influence someone using shopper principles to recruit others into considering purchasing our products.

Instead of talking about loyalty to the brand (by the consumer), this model invites you to consider loyalty to the shopper (by the brand/retailer). Instead of E-CRM – electronic customer relationship marketing – this model invites you to consider I-SRM – integrated shopper relationship marketing.

Why You Should Like This Model

Going back to the start of this chapter when we discussed the limitations of the linear model, we also talked about how all models were flawed. And while that's true, this consumer-shopper-consumer model is less flawed than traditional linear models.

Plus, there are a number of key attributes this model has in its favour:

– Closing the loop
This circular model gives you a line of sight from consumer to prospect through to shopper, consumer, loyal shopper and advocate. It reflects that these behaviours are continuous, repeated and circular. The value of this is that this model helps us think beyond each campaign and how we build value over the long term between the shopper and consumer and the brand or retailer.

– KPIs
Within each phase of the model we have suggested key channels, but whatever the channels that make most sense to your business, there are KPIs we can associate with each phase.

Awareness KPI: Reach
Path To Purchase KPI: Value

E-commerce & In Store KPI: Sales
Consumer Use KPI: Engagement
Advocacy & Loyalty KPI: Love

And because we can assign these KPIs, we can identify the metrics that we can measure in each channel, allowing us to develop and ROI model for each part of the consumer-shopper-consumer lifecycle.

This ability to clearly understand what the indicators of success are and how we measure them makes it easier for you and your teams to decide with digital marketing strategies and technologies to test and scale to get the best results for your business.

– Shopper Messaging
Because we put the shopper mind-set at the heart of this model (rather than centring it around the brand or the retailer), it makes it easy to remember the importance to use this model to consider what kind of shopper messages we can deliver at each part of the consumer-shopper lifecycle.

To figure out the correct shopper messaging, we need to ask first what we want the shopper to think at each phase of the model – let's use fish fingers as an example:

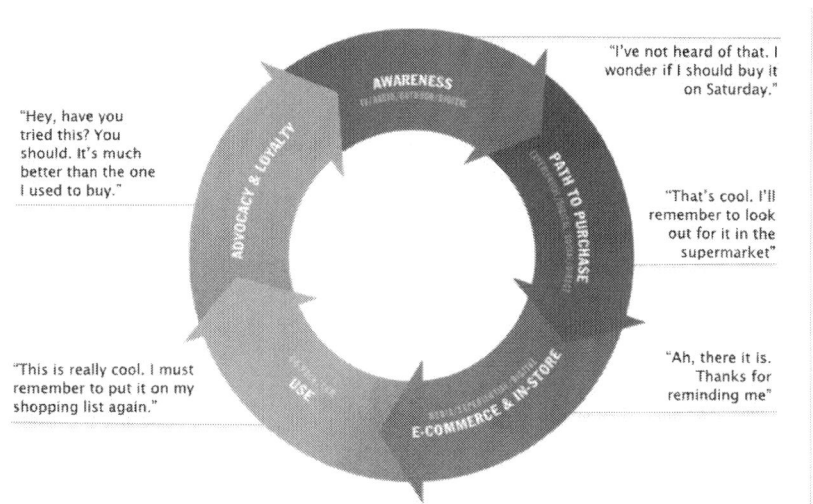

Now we can move on to consider some suitable shopper messages for each phase:

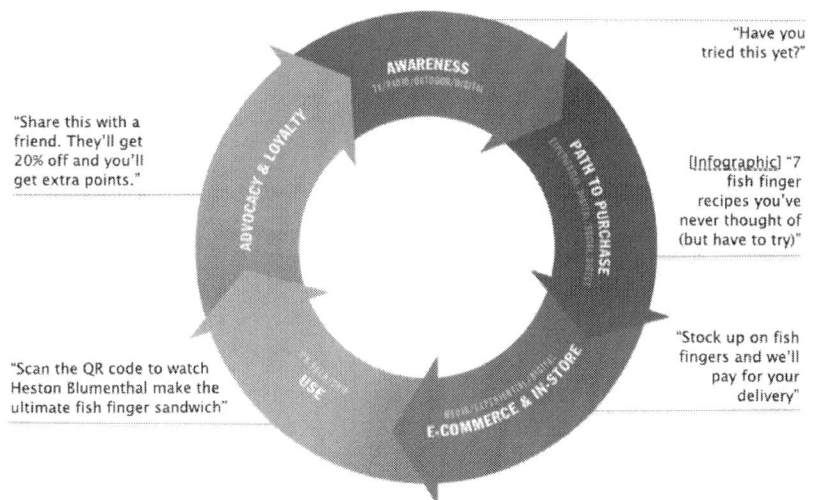

Notice that we can talk to people in a shopper mind-set in each stage of the lifecycle journey. So, for example, a social media post in the Awareness phase might say something like "Like if you love fish fingers." The Awareness is driven by friends of the liker seeing that they have Liked the post.

If we now switch the messaging to something that gets people to consider a purchase, the friends of the liker, commenter or sharer will see the post and be asked to consider purchasing. For example, "Have you tried these new fish fingers yet?" gets you to think about trial, a shopper mind-set focused activity.

– It's integrated

I suspect that marketers use the word *integrated* more than any other industry. And when it came to writing this section, I had to look up a few dictionary definitions to check how many of us use the word every day and what the word might actually mean. Here's a definition:

Integrated:

1. Combining or co-ordinating separate elements so as to provide a harmonious, integrated whole.

2. Organized or structured so that constituent units function co-operatively.

In systems engineering, a definition might be defined as:

The process of bringing together the component subsystems into one system and ensuring that subsystems function together as a system.

Here are two definitions of integrated marketing:

The application of consistent brand messaging across both traditional and non-traditional marketing channels, reinforcing each other.

Strategy aimed at unifying different marketing methods such as mass marketing, one-to-one marketing and direct marketing. Its objective is to complement and reinforce the market impact of each method.

Notice the recurring themes of focusing on the elements, units, and methods of a system. These descriptions make perfect sense in a pre-digital world where a shopper or consumer's interaction with a channel might well be a separate unit that is part of a larger system.

Go back a couple of decades (or more) and you may well have a large proportion of your target market who is sitting in front of their TV watching your advert, then after five to ten views they add your product to their shopping list, or decide to visit your store.

Even with the birth of the internet, you could conceive of a subset of your target audience only seeing your ads and communications in online banner ads, because they spend all their time on their computers rather than watching TV.

In these examples, you have defined channels that can be used to reach the target audience, and perhaps little crossover. This concept of channel definition has remained, baked into our models that allow the traditional funnel models of the shopper-consumer lifecycle. As we've already mentioned, this out-dated model suggests that if someone starts life as a prospect, we can drive awareness with above-the-line media, then they are taken to a second step where we use digital, experiential, social or direct marketing to interact with the prospect.

In this case, the definition of *Combining or co-ordinating separate elements so as to provide a harmonious, integrated whole* makes sense. It just doesn't reflect the complexity of a real digitally enabled world.

There's a definition of *integrated* that I prefer, and it comes from adapting a definition of social integration:

Social integration: A dynamic and principled process where all members participate in dialogue to achieve and maintain peaceful social relations.

Notice no mention of separate elements or units. This definition focuses on fluid processes and relationships. If I were to re-write this a little to suggest a new definition for integrated marketing in a digital world, it might read something like:

Integrated marketing: A dynamic and principled process using a number of marketing channels to enable all members to participate in dialogue to maximise and maintain value and utility.

To me, this means that brands and retailers use integrated marketing to focus less on channels and phases of marketing and specific methods, but on the overall goal of creating a unified or complimentary marketing mix. This process, no matter what the elements and steps in that process are for each consumer and shopper, seeks to maximise and maintain brand value, retailer value, shopper value and consumer value.

Integrated means understanding that we cannot control the channels that shoppers and consumers use, but instead aim to maximise the value that is transferred in whichever channels are used.

Integrated means that sometimes mass market channels are used to broadcast a message and sometimes one to one and direct comms are used to engage and provoke a two-way dialogue.

Integrated means that the just is not necessarily linear, with people moving from awareness to the path to purchase to sale to loyalty and advocacy. Some people will stay in a phase for a long time; others will progress quickly. Some will move forward through the model, then back again. Some will flit between the consumer and shopper mind-set many times. Some will only see comms in one channel; some will see comms in many channels.

Integrated means accepting all of the uncertainty above and responding with a marketing campaign or an always-on solution that might have comms that look like matching luggage, or might have complementary but channel-specific messaging.

This new integrated puts the person, rather than the brand, at the centre of the consumer-shopper lifecycle because this is the only way to consider all marketing in a digitally enabled world. A person will model from one phase of the model to the next if they perceive sufficient value in the brand or retailer that suits their current mind-set.

I hope this model, while not perfect, is the best fit to help you achieve your marketing and business objectives. This new definition of *integrated* helps the shopper and consumer make better decisions (in favour of your business).

The Right Message, Right Time (Re-visited)

We've already discussed the value of focusing on using the right message, at the right time, delivered to the right people, in the right context with the right level of personalisation.

Traditional consumer-shopper lifecycle models suggest a prescriptive approach to messaging, as those models suggest that you focus on the channel the messaging will go into – which means that social media, for example, is often seen as a channel for brand awareness.

Putting the shopper and consumers at the heart of our lifecycle allows us to think much more about how a person could come across that social media message in either a consumer or a shopper mind-set. They might have no awareness of your product or retailer, or they might be an advocate. They might have seen this message in a path to purchase phase, or post-purchase.

Recognising the complexity of the lifecycle means that while we may not always be able to show a message targeted both to that person, the mind-set they are in and where they are in the lifecycle, but at the least it makes us consider the appropriateness of that message for more than one context. This thinking will allow us to make our messaging more efficient.

Mission Shops And Mission Marketing

As we've already explored, traditional consumer-shopper lifecycle models tend to (deliberately or accidentally) position brand at the centre of the universe.

Our model encourages us to place the shopper at the heart of the model. I like to call this lens *having a single shopper view*. This view allows us to move from discussing marketing strategy at the level of an integrated model, through channels and then a comms strategy, to having a fascinating alternate starting point: a single consumer or shopper and their personal shopper mission.

Imagine I'm in the centre of Brighton with my five-year-old son Jasper and we're heading home to eat dinner. I was planning to heat up what's left over of last night's pasta for him. But Jasper's not been that hungry and is a bit picky today and I'd like him to eat a lot for dinner to make up for it.

So I ask him what he'd most like to eat for dinner. He says, "Fish fingers." So I decide to pop into the Tesco Metro on the way home to get him some fish fingers, because I know there are only two left in the packet at home. I prefer to buy Bird's Eye and I prefer the ones with Omega 3 added.

So I have a very specific mission that we can map against the messaging strategy: right message, at the right time, in the right place, with the right context and the right level of personalisation.

By focusing on the single shopper view – what some agencies are starting to describe as Mission Marketing – it allows us to sense check an integrated shopper campaign against not just a traditional planning approach to deliver the right messages in the right channels, but against some qualitative examples – a single shopper with a single mission. With this focus, we can see if the campaign actually works with real-world shoppers with real-world barriers and triggers to purchase.

As I stopped for a coffee earlier with Jasper, I checked my Facebook and saw a sponsored post for new Bird's Eye Wholegrain fish fingers. There was a promotional offer mentioned in the post and a call to action to add these new fish fingers to my Ocado shopping basket straight away. Thinking that I might as well try fish fingers that are the same ones Jasper likes, but with a new wholemeal crumb, I added them to my Ocado basket in a couple of clicks.

Now as I walk towards the Tesco Metro store, my phone vibrates in my pocket. I see a notification from Tesco offering my 50p off Bird's Eye Wholegrain Fish Fingers if I buy them in the Tesco store in front of me in the next 30 minutes. It's an offer for the same fish fingers that I was thinking about buying anyway, so I walk into the convenience store, pick up the fish fingers from the freezer, and scan my mobile voucher at the self scan machine on the way out.

I've saved 50p. My son loves them, so I feel like I've been a good parent. I've accomplished my very specific mission. Tesco and Ocado are happy because they have acquired more data about what I like to buy, when and where and the likelihood of me responding to an offer as I'm carrying out my varying mission shops.

Now what Tesco and Ocado can do is aggregate all the data on people who had added those fish fingers to their Ocado basket, and then who saw the mobile geo-located message. They can segment that data and use it to test future messages to send me when I'm close to a Tesco store, to see if they can influence other behaviour of mine, whether I'm on a mission shop or simply passing by.

What is perhaps most valuable about using the lens of mission marketing is that we can very quickly use digital tactics and strategy to move along the 70/20/10 rule.

If we are committed to spending 10% of resources on true innovation, we want to be able to get results fast and either write off an approach or make it much more efficient during the 20% phase, so ultimately we can see if that approach has the ability to become one that becomes part of our 70% core strategies – something proven and scalable.

When you're working on innovative digital strategies, it can be hard at first to pull out meaningful data in the ways that we may be used to. The number of users activated may be small and may not fully test a hypothesis, or shoppers may not do what we expect them to, leaving the top-level data looking incomplete.

But if you're collecting data that allows you to drill down into a single shopper view, even if your sample size is small, you'll be able to drill down into a handful of users to piece together what's really going on in the lives of your shoppers – their mission shops.

This deep dive analysis into the data will allow you to make some hypotheses that can be tested with your next marketing experiment. Often, planning to gather single shopper view data in advance of running a 10% experiment will make the difference between knowing what to do next when the experiment ends and not having a clue.

This process helps you focus on making shoppers' existing missions into more seamless and valuable experiences.

Who Made The Sale?

Sadie wants to buy a pair of trainers. She's been stopping and looking in shop windows now and again over the past few months, and sees a couple of pairs of purple trainers she likes the look of. When the sole starts coming off the bottom of her existing trainers, she decides she really needs to buy a new pair with her next paycheck.

So at lunchtime at work, she opens Firefox on her work computer and types in *buy trainers* into Google. At the top of the search result is an advert for ASOS. She clicks the link and visits the site and flicks through a few pages of trainers. There's a purple pair she likes and an orange pair too, so she adds both to her cart as she's already got an account with ASOS, and when it comes to payday, she can return to the site and choose which pair to buy then.

The next day Sadie is on Facebook on her mobile while on the bus home. As she's scrolling through the newsfeed, she sees an ad for the purple pair of trainers that she was looking at. The ad says there's a £5 voucher off a future purchase if she buys the trainers. She hadn't seen that offer before, so she clicks the Facebook ad and it takes her back to the ASOS product page. "Sod it," she thinks, "I'll buy them now and get them before payday." The next day, her purple trainers arrive and she feels awesome wearing them in the gym at the weekend.

Now here's the question: What caused Sadie to buy the trainers?

Was it the browsing in store? Or the ads?

And which ad facilitated the sale?

Was it the first Google Search ad? Or was it the Facebook re-targeting ad?

You're saying, *all of the above*, right?
Which is of course how we might rationally conclude when we're told the story of Sadie and her journey from awareness down the path to purchase to sale.

A funny thing happens in marketing teams (still all too often) when we get the reams of data back from our latest campaign. Many people attribute the sale to the last click. In this case, *last click attribution* would credit the re-targeting ad with making the sale.

But that might not tell the full picture. For all we know, the Google Search campaign might have been failing. Perhaps it was targeting the wrong keywords or the ads were bought at the wrong price, or they were targeting the wrong demographics.

And perhaps that re-targeting ad was successful in converting people to buy, but there were so few people in the sales pipeline at that stage that it hardly mattered. If you focus on last click attribution, the answer might be to continue with Facebook re-targeting, and increase the scope, so that all actions on the website are re-targeted.

This would be a mistake, as the traffic source – Google Search – for the keywords *buy trainers* is not providing the right clicks at the right price. But perhaps re-targeting people who visit the ASOS website from natural search listings would be much more profitable. Or re-targeting people who open email offers are more profitable. Or re-targeting Google Search queries, but only from mobile users, would give better results.

If you only get last click attribution analytics, you'll never know. That's why you need to spend time with your team to develop a solid attribution data.

I know, I know. Attribution is not sexy. It's boring. And hard. And it involves lots of data. Which is why when the data people pull out interesting insights, it often doesn't lead CMOs to think, "That was great; we must do more media attribution", but instead, "That was great, let's run more re-targeting ads."

But I would like to briefly make the case for focusing on attribution rather than *last click* data, as it's probably the most important thing you can do once you've pushed the big *Go* button on your campaign.

Here's why:

1. Proper attribution gives credit to the supporting media.

Focusing only on the last click before conversion is like crediting the till in a store for the sale. It's as silly as only crediting the A-frame sign outside the shop with the sale and ignoring all your above-the-line, below-the-line communications and ignoring the in-store signage and store staff.

2. Proper attribution reflects the multi-channel world.

Because it's easy to shift from one device to another – researching trainers at work on a laptop to continuing to check the website on your phone on the bus, to showing your partner on a tablet at home – it also needs to be our goal to track that entire multi-channel journey. It's hard, yes, and attribution experts don't have all the answers. But it is getting easier.

3. Proper attribution keys your brand in pole position

If you only look at the last click before conversion, you do not understand the increasingly complex marketing mix that leads to a successful sale, which means you'll not be able to adjust your spending intelligently and with all the facts at hand. This will lead to more wastage. And if your competitors are attributing correctly and you're not, they're in a good position to jostle you and your brand out of the way – not necessarily with better campaigns, or a better offering, or even a large spend, but with better data insights with which to plan the next campaign.

Step 2 Key Points:
Owning The Path To Purchase

• Shoppers do not shop like a linear model, from awareness to the path to purchase to sale to loyalty and advocacy. Some will stay in a phase for a long time; others progress quickly. Some flit between the consumer and shopper mind-set many times.

• The Consumer-Shopper Lifecycle Model puts shopper mind-set at the heart of our thinking. It recognises the path to purchase as an important phase in the lifecycle, but also recognises other (often overlooked) phases as equally important.

The five key stages of the Consumer-Shopper Lifecycle:

- Awareness
- Path To Purchase
- E-commerce & In Store
- Consumer Use
- Loyalty & Advocacy

Consumer-Shopper Lifecycle Model benefits:

• Gives line of sight from consumer to prospect, to shopper, consumer, loyal shopper and advocate. It reflects that these behaviours are continuous, repeated and circular.

• The model helps us think beyond each campaign and how we build value over the long term between the shopper and consumer and the brand or retailer.

• Because we put the shopper mind-set at the heart of this model (rather than the brand or the retailer), it makes it easy to remember to consider what kind of shopper messages we can deliver at each part of the consumer-shopper lifecycle.

- We can very quickly use digital tactics and strategy to move along the 70/20/10 rule.

Jobs To Be Done:

- Discuss the Consumer-Shopper Lifecycle Model with your team – how can it work for you and put the shopper at the heart of your integrated approach?

- Discuss the pros and cons of campaigns versus an *always on* approach.

- Discuss how mission marketing and a single shopper view might influence your marketing strategy.

- Review your media attribution process

Step 3:

Hacking The In-Store Experience

The first time I visited Hamleys, I didn't see any staff.

It might have been that they were there, but I just didn't notice them because I was so absorbed in the sheer volume and selection of toys. I think I was eight or nine, and Hamleys was heaven.

Growing up in Yeovil, where the best toy store was a section of a small local department store chain in a sleepy market town, any decent size toy store was a revelation. Trips to Exeter to go to Gamleys always seemed to be too short, no matter how long I was allowed to wander the aisles and play.

So a trip to Hamleys was intense. I thought, *Why doesn't our town have this?* and *How did I not know about all these toys before?* I remembered that they had the full range of everything (or, at least, that's how it seemed to me). I loved Star Wars, and the shelves had dozens of different figures, instead of 10 or 20. The more obscure action play sets were there too, not just an At-At and Jabba The Hut's Palace.

But I never once noticed the staff. Which seems odd to me, as Hamleys is five minutes' walk from my office now, and I go there several times a year to buy presents. The first thing I notice now is the awesome staff. They are at the entrance welcoming me and demonstrating bubble guns or boomerang planes or UFO-shaped balloons. They are on every floor demonstrating quadcopters and magic pens and magic tricks.

Outside of the US, they are the most enthusiastic, friendly and happy sales staff you'll ever see. When I visit the store now, the huge selection of toys is a pleasure to look at, but I've since been to FAO Schwartz and I've long since gotten used to the endless shelves of Amazon. Plus, I guess adults see the world with less wide-eyed enthusiasm. So, now it's the staff that makes Hamleys such a magical place for me now.

Digital Disruption And The In-Store Experience

The retail experience is hugely important. Up to 76% of purchase decision happens in store (according to Popai, 2012). You can spend all you like on advertising, but if three-quarters of the purchase decision is made in store, you better get that store experience right for each shopper.

In retail terms, the Hamleys experience is made up of:

- Retail design
- Space planning
- Range
- Retail displays
- Staff knowledge and customer service

These are all things with a tangible output that can be measured in the retail environment.

- Is the shelf well stocked?
- Are the staff well trained?
- Is the store easy to navigate?

So how can digital help in this environment, when the rules that govern it are so simple, practical and physical?

The answer is that digital needs to be employed (appropriately, and alongside more traditional methods) to enhance and innovate the customer experience.

And it's essential. And it's essential to do right now.

Here's the problem: It doesn't sound like it's essential to do now. It sounds soft and fluffy. Especially to retailers, who are used to talking about sales per metre and width of aisles and planograms and staff incentivised sales. Who needs an enhanced customer experience? Sounds like something a fluffy marketing agency would come up with...

In 2014, when Amazon announced they were investigating drone deliveries, it sounded like an April Fools' Day joke. Then the retailer got approval from the Federal Aviation Administration to start testing drones. Then in 2015, Amazon released this footage of a new type of drone: https://www.youtube.com/watch?v=MXo_d6tNWuY

In 2015, Amazon and Google and Instacart and others made one-hour delivery of items the standard in Silicon Valley. Now Amazon believes that drones can make some delivery times as short as 15 minutes.

When I can order online and receive a delivery in 15 minutes, what is the point of a physical retail store?

I mean, let's think about it for a minute. Brick and mortar stores first existed as the only place to go and buy the things you needed. Now that e-commerce is all grown up, year after year the post-Christmas shopping stories report that online sales are up and High Street sales are down.

But even up until 2014, you could argue, "Well, what if I need a pint of milk right now, I can't order that from Amazon, can I?!" And then along came Amazon Fresh with one-hour delivery. So, if in the next couple of years, one-hour and sub-one-hour deliveries become the norm to most towns and cities, where does that leave brick and mortar stores? What is the point of their expensive retail estate and high overheads and shelves and staff and limited shelf space?

And that's how we get to customer experience.

Because what we have left once e-commerce delivers on the practical factors of shopping such as range, cost, convenience and speed of delivery, is customer experience.

People will always love shopping.

Shopping as therapy.

Shopping as a social activity.

Shopping to feel good.

Shopping where you can touch and feel that cashmere sweater, where you can demo and hear that Sonos speaker, where you can sample Morrisons' bread freshly baked in store four times a day.

E-commerce can never come close in these areas. Which gives us a place to look for how we can appropriately use digital to innovate in the customer experience.

Experience Beats Product

Three in four millennials (78%) would choose to spend money on an experience or event over buying something desirable [source: Harris Associates, 2015].

This love of experience over things is most pronounced in millennials, but not exclusive to that age group. In surveys, all age groups value experiences over things.

The funny thing is, many retailers act like the opposite is true. When grocery retailers are locked in an on-going price war, there's a fine line between competitive advantage to gain customers and a pyrrhic victory in a race to the bottom. And since the financial crash set in motion in 2007, it's not just grocery retail that's seen a renewed focus on pricing and value.

For consumers, value is everywhere in retail, from cut-price Subway sandwiches to Black Friday sales that place discounts at the start of the biggest spending season. But is value pricing really the driver we all think it is?

Listen To The Science, Not The Market

The science of happiness that says that people derive more happiness from spending on experience than products. Buy a new pair of jeans, and you get a short-term high, but your happiness levels soon return to baseline, while you risk buyer's remorse.

Buy an experience, like a holiday, and you value it for a much longer term. Part of this is because you get to anticipate it, which delivers as much happiness as the event itself, according to studies. Then you have the memories to re-live, which generates more happiness. Then you have the experience itself.

But what does this have to do with CPG or retail marketing? Experiences make a product more valuable. Delivering a better brand experience makes shoppers assign more value to that product – not value created by price, but value associated by elevating a product from just another thing we can buy to something that delivers a premiumness or an everyday luxury from the experience of it.

According to a survey of 1,000 UK shoppers by retail marketing agency **Live & Breathe**, 34% want a better in store experience, while 1 in 5 (18%) think that the shopping experience on the High Street is getting worse (rising to 21% of 25- to 34-year-olds).

We need to fix this.

We can take a lesson from the rise of Starbucks. When the coffee chains first appeared on the High Street, they delivered a superior coffee to UK's cafes. But they also delivered an experience. They brought your living room into the High Street with comfy sofas and a sense that we were living inside an episode of *Friends* – where a High Street store was not just a place to hurry past, but to pause, relax, chat and people watch. That experience of the retail environment is inseparable from the cup of coffee. The vast majority of the value of a £3 cup of coffee comes from the in-store experience.

This value of experience of a product is taken to the extreme by the fanboys and fangirls who create YouTube unboxing videos – showing, in exquisite detail, the opening up of a new product. From opening the beautiful packaging of a new iPhone, to cracking open a Kinder Egg to reveal the toy, unboxing fetishises the product to make it all about the experience. That's where the value lies.

The products we sell can be both *things* and *experiences* depending on how they are packaged, presented and the context in which they are used and consumed.

A strawberry might just be a *thing*, a commodity. A shopper's decision to buy them might be based on how much they and their family like strawberries and the current market price. It's a thing. But if you're using that strawberry on your child's fifth birthday cake for a party you've invited 30 kids to, that strawberry is a thing *and* it will play a role in an experience. If strawberries are really expensive this week due to a supply shortage, and your child loves strawberries and raspberries equally, you might buy raspberries, because both are still commodity products that you will make into part of an experience.

But take a single strawberry and place it on a plate at El Bulli, the world's most awarded restaurant, and it becomes an experience. When El Bulli was open, millions of people joined the waiting list to eat that strawberry, when there were just thousands of seats available. That strawberry was infused with gin and tonic and BBQ flavourings so that the drink flavours are tasted first, followed by the BBQ taste, and finally the strawberry itself. The dish was designed to evoke memories of summer BBQs. The commodity product is now undoubtedly an experience.

Of course we know this lesson about experiences intuitively. We know that a takeaway coffee savoured as you walk to a meeting might be less of a memorable experience than a coffee in a Starbucks on a brilliant first date – which in turn, might be less of an experience than a coffee at the end of a meal in a amazing restaurant to celebrate a job promotion.

So Why Aren't We Focused On In-Store Experiences?

The mistake that some CPG and retail brands make when thinking about how to add value to products is they see the brand as a tangible thing with value in and of itself. Because they work for the brand, they might overestimate the brand's value. Which is strange, because the brand is at worst an abstract construct, and at best a sum total of all customer experiences with the product or retailer.

Either way, the brand experience doesn't exist in the world; it exists in our heads. That's why we should focus on an individual's consumer experience of the brand, not on protecting the brand. Great customer service, personal service and personalisation are all great ways to turn a thing into an experience, protecting it from commoditisation.

When Nutella offered jars to be printed with personalised messages in Selfridges, there were long queues to buy a jar. Had that jar cost two, five or even ten times the standard prices, I bet there would still be people queuing up to buy.

The question is, how can we take advantage of the desire for experiences and re-work our product offering or our retail stores to create better experiences?

Starbucks Reserve in Covent Garden, London marries the power of the brand with the look and feel of a high-end private members' club. The copper funnels and glass siphons bring an old-fashioned craft element, while the hosts who greet you make you feel like you're in an independent restaurant where your custom is of paramount importance. It's about the experience. The coffee is just the product the experience is wrapped around.

It's easy to look at the flagship stores of luxury retailers such as Burberry or Nespresso to see how they zone the store and invest in attentive staff, great store design and helpful technology to build memorable experiences worth paying a premium price for. It's harder to suggest how to create the same effect in a sector that's used to focussing on price and value and convenience as its drivers.

What's Stopping Investment In Experiences?

There are two reasons:

1. Cash

and

2. Dogma

The economy grew 2.5% this year and 2016 is set to be the same. The challenge for retail in 2016 is how to grow in a cautious economy, while innovating in response to changing shopping behaviour. The High Street is being disrupted by changing shopping behaviour around which channels they shop in and how they use technology. That's a problem for physical stores, but moving towards more experiential stores is not necessarily the obvious answer when your industry is tied up in…

...Dogma is a challenge for retailers. Physical retail is being disrupted at such a pace by e-commerce and innovative new business models that it's hard for some retailers to keep up (hello Blockbusters, Virgin Megastores and Woolworths). But shops have always worked the same way, so do we really have to change now? Long rows of shelving make sense in a world where you have to shop in physical retail stores. But when e-commerce satisfies on the hygiene factors of ease of shop, range and price, physical retail stores need to do more. They need to offer experiences people can't get online – and not just the crap ones, such as standing in queues or meeting unhelpful staff.

The area stores can excel in is in providing an experience that is visually stunning and emotionally engaging. Virgin Holidays' new retail format V Room (in the image at the top of the post) is based on Virgin's airport lounges because *it's no longer good enough to just have a shop with brochures on a wall and sales people behind a desk.* You can experience a little bit of what it would be like to go on holiday to various destinations, by being given airport lounge service and served food from the country of your choice. It's a very different experience than being greeted by a salesperson behind a computer.

What About Sectors Where It's All About Value?
Even in grocery retail, there are some great examples of building premium experiences into grocery stores. Morrisons' Market Street counters encourage you to ask for advice and help from the in-house bakery, the butcher, fishmonger etc. They'll take the time to advise you and to extend your culinary skills while filleting your fish or preparing your meat just how you like it. The retailer's pizza counters allow you to create your own pizza from a choice on toppings, to take home.

Waitrose is trialling sushi bars where you can take away freshly made sushi, or sit at a stool and eat in. In the US, Wholefoods' spin-off chain 365 is introducing tattoo parlours and Bulletproof Coffee.

People say that grocery is all about price, range and convenience… but maybe customers are not as price sensitive as we think. Sure, there are plenty of households on a budget, but these same families will happily spend money on coffee and cake in Starbucks at the weekend or eating out.

Maybe by framing the conversation around price, we are training more and more grocery customers to compare grocers in this way. Perhaps there's another way.

While discounters such as Aldi and Lidl have grown by framing the conversation around price, Waitrose has weathered the storm by hardly entertaining that conversation. Waitrose has achieved its 91st consecutive period of growth – the longest current run of success for any supermarket, according to Kantar. It's easy to say that grocery is all about everyday low pricing. And it's easy to join that game. But the costs of playing that game with smaller retailers with lower cost bases are high.

By focussing on in-store experience instead, you invest in those experiences instead of price cuts. And as people value experiences more than things, it would be fascinating to see what the effect would be if a major supermarket adopted this approach. The question is: Is anyone brave enough to be an iconoclast and go against the grain of the received wisdom in this sector, despite what the science of happiness might say?

Physical Retailers Have A Choice To Make
At Galerie Lafayette in Paris, there is a Chanel store where you can't just walk in. You have to queue to gain access. The greeter at the door will ask you which items you want to browse before you are allowed in. Once inside, you feel lucky to be able to hold and touch the bags.

A few streets away, you might find a street seller hawking fake Chanel bags. He is selling them at a fraction of the price of the real bags. The quality is slightly less, and he is making a tiny profit margin on the bags, compared with the huge mark-up of the bags inside the Galerie Lafayette. But despite his value offering, there is no ten-minute queue. People are queuing for the brand experience that the Chanel store inside Galerie Lafayette offers. No one here is worrying about prices.

I know not all of our brands are Chanel, but that's not really the point. By focusing on price, we are setting the frame of experience of our retail or CPG brand around cost – around its pure utilitarian value. Instead, we could not do that. We could focus on engineering customer experiences around our brand so powerful that people want to have those experiences. They want to buy our brand at the prices we set because of how that experience makes us feel.

Digital Innovation To Enhance The Customer Experience
The message is clear: Create experiences in store that make people want to come back not because they have to go there to get their shopping done, but because they want to.

Here are a few beautiful in-store environments that combine retail innovation with digital to make for a stunning customer experience:

Whole Foods offer customers a way to discover new wines they'll like with this digital wine palette picker. What I really like is how the screen is cased within wood, housing the technology into the existing Wholefoods store design concepts.

These screens demand attention and can be used to run above-the-line and brand assets, or to quickly change the lighting of the store. You could say *technology's the new luxury* – a premium customer experience can be generated not only by luxury products and pricing, but by the smart use of digital technology.

I love this car showroom. The space is planned as a discovery space for potential buyers, with digital screens planned for from inception, rather than as an add-on.

This is a great example of how digital touchscreens can be used to remove counters and break down the barrier between staff and customers. Instead of being seated across a desk in a travel agent, while the customer service staff stare at a screen and tap at a keyboard, here customer and staff member can stand together browsing destinations and holiday options, mirroring how you might holiday search with a friend or family member at home on an iPad.

Digital fitting rooms still need to prove their value in High Street fashion. If executed clumsily, they can be a good example of technology needlessly getting in the way.

Do I really want to enter my Facebook details on a screen in a changing room to share my look on social media to get feedback? Here, this virtual fitting room allows the shopper to quickly try on lots of different outfits fast, without needing to get changed. The idea is not to replace the fun of browsing outfits on a rail or to remove the need for really trying on clothes, but to save precious minutes so you can spend more time with the small number of pieces you really like.

Often, to make technology part of a seamless experience in retail, you want to make the technology blend in to the surroundings, easy and intuitive to use and understand. Only occasionally do you want to make technology itself the hero.

And this is one of those times. This bar does away with the need for human bartenders, replacing him or her with a robot bartender who can mix you all cocktails ever conceived, including those you invent yourself on an iPad. By combining discovery through endless choice, perfection in cocktail execution, and the ability to personalise your drinks, the technology here makes up a huge part of the customers' experiences. The bar environment and range of drinks only needs to live up to the bar set by the technology.

Here Nike brings the online experience in store, with a number of computers pointing to Nike's website where you can completely design and personalise a pair of trainers, then buy them and ship them. Bringing the online experience in store is one of the most rewarding ways to get shoppers engaging with digital. Get it wrong, and you have a lot of screens with no one using them. Get it right and the sight of people sending chunks of time absorbed in an activity is highly seductive to other shoppers.

Nike innovating again. Social user generated content is curated alongside brand content on large screens in store. This curation works in two ways.

The user-generated content editorializes the brand content, giving breadth and depth to the ideas. The content from regular people provides *social proof* to shoppers – people advocating for and engaging with Nike tells the shoppers viewing these posts that other people like them should also like Nike.

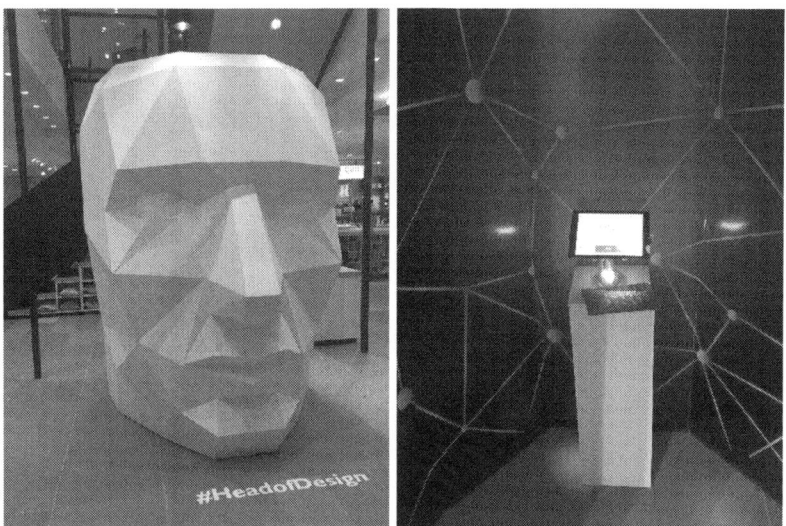

Department store House Of Fraser recognises the challenge of bringing online experiences in store, so it houses its home décor mood board tablet app inside a huge geometric head in the centre of the home furnishings floor.

Once you step inside, you're cocooned, giving you the time and space to play around with the app, which helps you create personalised moodboards and email them to yourself.

And finally, back to in-store six-sheets... this digital screen in Selfridges stands apart from most beauty concessions screens. Like other luxury retailers in the store, this screen shows clips of beautifully filmed above-the-line content of pouting models. But Nars have one eye on brand and another category sales, as the film content is interspersed with simple product imagery that showcases the range to shoppers at a distance.

Digital In Store Can Be Cheap And Simple

One of the biggest challenges with digital signage and other technology in store is that screens still don't come cheap. A screen might be pretty much the same as a big TV, but if you need one that can run all day every day and not break, they cost a little bit more than your home TV.

Many screen technology companies will let you lease tech or create a monthly payment plan out of an operational expenditure budget, so you don't have to ask the board for Cap Ex to add more digital to your store estate, but it's still a decent chunk of cash for many retailers.

Which is why I'm always on the lookout for ways to bring aspects of digital in store, or items that do the same job as big screens – grab attention – at a fraction of the cost.

The above example is genius in my opinion. Nordström simply attach cardboard and plastic signs to items that are highly Pinned on Pinterest. You get the power of social proof without any cost to bring technology in store.

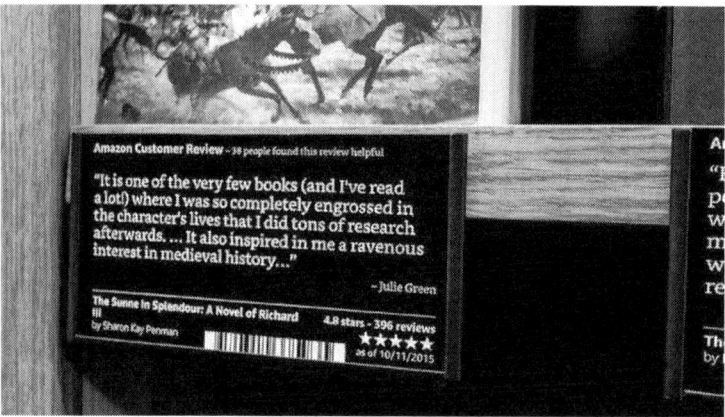

Amazon opened its first physical bookstore in November 2015, 20 years after Bezos' company started online. The two photos above show how Amazon can bring the value of its customer data into physical retail. The amalgamated ratings deliver powerful social proof, backed by the size of the data pool that rating represents. The cherry-picked customer review brings richness to the store. While these signs are cardboard, the technology needed to deliver the words on the cardboard is immense and invisible.

Technology doesn't always need to be cutting edge to stand out. This dot matrix screen acts as a ticker tape. But the movement catches your peripheral vision as you walk by, making you turn your head to look in the window. Not high-tech, but effective.

You might tell me that I can't really talk about lighting in a section about in-store technology, as this isn't really digital tech, but just some neon tubes. And that's exactly the point.

Much like the previous above, technology that gets attention doesn't need to be advanced, but effective. The interesting shape of the neon tubes framing the clothes in this shop window certainly stands out.

Digital For Hygiene

Most of the previous examples focus on digital signage and technology adding to the shopper experience through aesthetics. But that's not the only way digital can add value to the customer experience.

Digital technology can play a key role in the customer experience through enhancing hygiene factors such as ease of use, speed of delivery, range and cost.

Here, this screen is not being used for aesthetics, but for the practical purpose of directing shoppers entering the store to the right floor. And because it's a screen, rather than cardboard, the sign can animate to draw attention to itself, in order to make shoppers' visits easier. Notice that rather than just using words, photos of the current range are also included to entice shoppers in.

Sainsbury's tablet attached to a trolley is one example of how supermarkets are thinking about how to innovate the customer experience to make it easier for them to shop. Some grocers and other large retailers are looking at how to make navigating a store easier. Using beacons at shelf to communicate the precise location of different categories, a shopper would be able to enter their shopping list in an app or query individual items, and be led to the items in the most efficient, time-saving route possible.

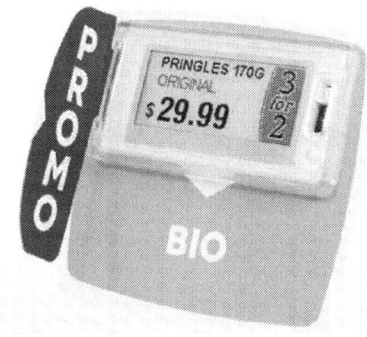

Shelf edge labels are yet to move beyond limited trials in UK retailers. But their utility to the shopper and the retailer means their time will come. The latest shelf edge labels allow pricing to be shown as well as other text, such as offers, brand messages, and flashing imagery to grab attention.

Prices can also be updated by head office or at shelf very quickly, meaning that prices can be adjusted according to competitor pricing, popularity and stock levels. Labels like the above combine digital e-paper screens alongside printed glorifiers, making the most of both old and new technology.

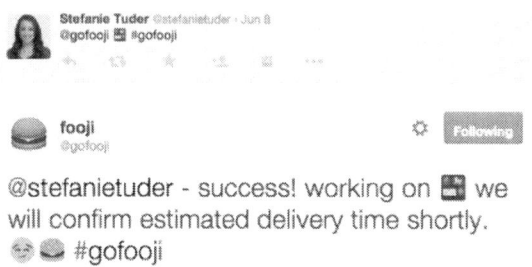

Emojis might at first seem like a hugely disruptive communication tool, but companies like Fooji are using emojis to make ordering takeaway as easy as ordering an Uber car.

You text or tweet an emoji of the food you want, and for a flat fee of $15, Fooji selects a nearby restaurant to make your food and has it delivered. The service (at the end of 2015) is in a handful of US cities, but it's an interesting idea to examine if consumers really do want endless choice, or whether hygiene factors such as ease of use and speed of delivery are a way of grabbing a significant market share of the food delivery market.

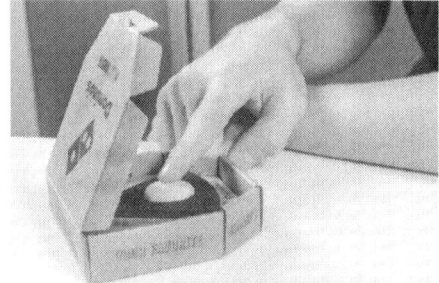

Dominos is taking online food ordering to the ultimate level of convenience with this single button that you can keep next to your remote controls for the ultimate *Netflix and chill* evenings.

This button is connected to an app via Bluetooth, where you store your favourite pizza combination. When you press the button, your pizza is ordered and your bank account charged – all with the single push of a button.

These buttons are being trialled in 2016, and you can certainly see the logic of focusing on convenience of ordering. Domino's currently receives 75% of all its orders digitally – up from 41% of orders in 2011 – with 50% of those being placed via mobile. Its app has accumulated 10 million downloads. And while this single button isn't the answer to how everyone wants to order pizza, *superfans* with a high order frequency will no doubt value convenience as a hygiene factor.

Which Lens: Business Vs. Shopper?

Unless you're a retailer with unlimited budgets, you'll want to develop a rationale for which aspects of innovation and digital technology you want to implement into your stores.

We've already looked at using the 70/20/10 model to identify which aspects of digital to trial and then scale with your team, but when it comes to signing off capital expenditure budgets to change the retail store environment, you might find yourself looking for an explicit lens through which to make your purchasing recommendations.

The three clearest ways I've found to make a case for buying in-store digital:

1. Cost Efficiencies & Revenue Generation
While in-store technology is still expensive relative to print, over the long term, there is a business case to make where replacing print with screens can be cost effective – and revenue generating.

While the cost of a printed six sheet is small, multiplied by a large store estate, and multiplied by many campaigns over times, digital starts to look interesting. Content can be displayed on digital six sheets without printing and logistics costs.

The site can also be sold to supplier brands and partners as a media space, creating a new revenue stream.

2. Marketing Efficiency

The trouble with print is how long it takes to change it to suit consumer demand, time of day, requirements of the campaign, etc. Take the media spaces below, for example. The ads in these spaces are a poor use of space. The top ad for a meal deal makes less sense early in the morning and will be most effective during lunchtime, becoming less effective at driving sales after that. The bottom ad for the wine deal will be most effective to drive sales during the evening commute.

If we made the case for swapping these two ads for a single digital screen, we'd allow for speedier updating of content, so we could change the message to suit day part, thereby making the media and the ad site more effective and efficient.

You now free up space, allowing you to rotate more than one message on a single ad site. And you can also split test a campaign creative to see which is most effective in driving sales. Does a small red circle with the offer make more sales versus a red circle twice the size? These learnings from split testing can be applied to all future ad creatives. If we test, test, test and apply the learnings, we can rapidly increase the efficiency of our ads.

There are also other advantages to digital screens over print, when it comes to efficiency to advertising to convert to sale. Many screens can run weather-dependent messages – e.g. a sausage brand could run different ads depending on the temperature of a summer's day – if it's hot, run the ads about sausages on the barbecue; if it's colder than expected, run ads about sausages grilled at home.

Some digital screens now offer basic face recognition and claim to be able to run ads depending on whether there are more male or female faces. Personally, I'm not convinced of the value of this feature. A retailer or brand knows its audience, so the chances of its audience changing that dramatically to warrant a different ad creative for men or women at a specific ad hoarding seems slim.

Newer digital ad shells turn the screen into a giant computer, allowing for content to be delivered differently for each screen in an estate, and for that content to be updated in real time. That means you can call out location ("Hello Bristol shoppers…"), provide useful details, such as a map to the nearest store, or update content in real time, such as latest social media posts and reviews, or a countdown clock, counting down to an event such as Mother's Day.

All these innovations allow our advertising messages to be tailored and targeted to time of day and local preferences and environments. That, combined with split testing and measuring against sales uplift in a location, makes digital screen media a huge opportunity to make our ad money go further by testing what works to drive sales.

3. Brand Experience
When we're creating ads for digital screens, it's easy to focus on the specific role of the communication. But there's another role that digital screen ads can fulfill because of the ability to change them to suit times of day, and different local audiences. That role is brand experience in stores.

How can we tailor digital ads to give shoppers a better experience? By making sure that content doesn't just deliver messages around price, range, promotions and convenience, but by talking to specific groups of people at specific times to give them a brand experience that better fits their specific needs.

Print requires that you talk to the majority of your brand or retail audience with a message that is most likely to interest people in your product or brand. A frozen fish finger brand, for example, talks to families, mums and dads who buy the food. But a digital screen can allow for multiple messages. If you know that young mums are shopping in greater numbers at 3-4pm on weekdays, and at 9am shoppers have a greater proportion of senior citizens, then your digital screen can create messages that are tailored to these audiences and their needs.

This means that the brand can target messages to distinct segments in both overt and subtle ways to increase the quality of the experience individuals have in store.

Using Mobiles In Store

If we loved a person as much as our mobiles, we'd be labelled lovesick, or obsessed. If you've ever felt anxious or panicky when you've lost or been without your mobile, then you're in the two-thirds of us who struggle to imagine life without a mobile phone.

But, imagine yourself in a supermarket with a mobile phone and what do you picture? Scanning a QR code to find out baked bean recipes? Nope. Downloading an augmented reality app to watch a bottle of juice animate and explode with juiciness? No, us neither.

And that's the dilemma. Mobile phones are essential in every key area of life. The one area that lags behind is using mobile phones in store – especially when grocery shopping. But that is changing. A 2014 survey by IGD shows 60% of shoppers don't have a useful grocery app, but 72% say they have apps from other retailers they find useful. Perhaps this is why only 4% do grocery shopping on a mobile phone, but 32% buy from other retail sectors online.

In order for brands and retailers to keep pace with change and enable better applications for shoppers to use their mobile phones in store, we need to invest in the following areas:

1. Mobile couponing.
The vast majority of grocery checkouts in grocery stores aren't able to scan through the glass on mobile phones. The cost to upgrade is not insignificant, but if we invest, the mobile path to purchase becomes seamless and will drive brand sales. In non-grocery stores, companies like Eagle Eye enable digital couponing at till, creating a seamless journey from advertising an offer (by email, or Facebook perhaps), to redeeming the digital offer in store.

2. Mobile payments
With Apple Pay and a number of competitors looking to turn contactless payment into something you do with your phone rather than your card, we need to embrace this and speed up convenience checkouts in particular. In the US, Walmart along with other retailers are snubbing Apple Pay for their own QR code payment system.

3. Wi-Fi store
Wi-Fi in store eventually rolled out in Waitrose and Morrisons in 2014 (Tesco led the way in 2011). In the wider High Street retailer estate, accessing free Wi-Fi in some retailers is so painful it's easier not to bother. We need to make this work better, so that if people want to use their mobiles to browse online product reviews, they can.

4. Beacons
The main grocers have done trials, but supplier brands are keen to use beacon proximity messaging as a media services channel. A number of UK High Street retailers have tentatively trialled beacon messaging, but it's yet to be fully embraced by retailers or the public. Retailers thinking of how to use beacon messaging need to manage the balance between spamming shoppers and opening up a powerful new messaging opportunity.

5. Mobile apps in store (and out)
In grocery, there is no killer retail app that is driving adoption of mobile app use in 2016, either in or outside of store. This needs to change. This could be an e-commerce app that focuses more on shoppers' lifestyle needs around different shops or shopping lists. Or it could be an app that helps shoppers navigate and find products, find complimentary products and recipes, and build shopping lists. The link between a retail app and the in-store retail experience is yet to be made successfully.

Beacons: The New In-store Announcements Or The New QR Codes?

Beacons are one of the most recent technologies that promise to disrupt the in-store retail environment.

On one hand they sound like the holy grail of shopper marketing: cost-effective, targeted, segmented, localised, personalised timely messages. You can drive offers, prevent showrooming, and even follow up with shoppers after they leave the store. Beacons are small devices you can stick on a wall in a store, shopping centre or entertainment venue that can talk to phones up to 70 metres away. They don't need an internet connection, they don't need a plug, and the batteries last three years.

Current mobile marketing models are broken. Beacons promise to fix the problem. According to new research from retail IT specialist Imerja, more than 80% of UK shoppers say that retailers aren't doing enough to make them feel like an individual when shopping in store. Beacons are one strategy that can reduce this figure.

On the other hand, beacons have been around for a couple of years and have yet to fulfil their promise. When some retailers and brands still can't get email working right, what chance have we got to send shoppers messages that they want on their mobiles when they are in store, rather than ones that are just intrusive and spammy?

If we get beacons wrong, they run the risk of becoming the next QR code – a technology with great promise that never worked out.

Beacons. iBeacons. Bluetooth beacons. Proximity-based targeting. Whatever you call it, beacons offer a neat way of sending messages to shopper's mobiles as they walk around a store.

Beacons have been successfully trialled in a shopping centre in Eastleigh, Hampshire, by Coke at the World Cup, by Virgin Atlantic, Eat and William Hill. The idea is that you download the brand or retailer's app, turn on your smartphone's Bluetooth and then you receive targeted timely Push messages on your phone (with no further prompting from the user) in and around the retail environment.

When Beacons Go Wrong

One of the first major retail developments using beacons in the UK was in June 2014. Regent Street was going to be kitted out with beacons, as part of a £1 billion Regent Street modernisation program by the Crown Estate.

So see how the beacons were working from a shopper's perspective, I make four different trips to see the beacons in action. One hundred of the street's stores including Burberry, Banana Republic and Hugo Boss had the beacons installed in their entrances, with another 30+ stores due to join in over the following months.

Before my first visit, I downloaded the Regent Street app advertised on banners in the street and buses. The app invites you to *thumb up* or *thumb down* brands and interests (so I give everything a thumbs up), which should trigger any messages and offers set up by those 100 retailers when I come within a 100-metre range of their doorways.

The only problem is, the magic didn't happen. I spent three-quarters of an hour in Hamley's looking for a toy for my son, 15 minutes in Burberry browsing shirts and jackets, then into Superdry looking for holiday shorts.

Not once was I invited to get 3-for-2 deal on Hackett Polo shorts or invited to try delicious paninis and sandwiches at Starbucks (as a blogger reported). Maybe I was unlucky and there were no offers at the times of day I visited. Maybe there was a technical issue.

But not getting any messages on my phone screen was not the biggest issue with the beacons project.

There was a key element missing from making an innovative beacons implementation work – there was a lack of awareness. Sure, there were some out-of-home posters telling shoppers to download the Regent Street app, but there was absolutely to mention of why you should download the app – to receive timely and personalised offers from stores as you shopped. There were no signs in the stores talking about the app or the beacon messaging. Nothing.

While it was impressive to see beacons trialled at such scale, what I learned is that in order to stand a good chance of making beacon messaging work, you need scale. You need lots of people downloading the app. And lots of people knowing that if they do they will get a better deal or exclusive offers. The technology doesn't do that job on its own. Beacons marketing is only likely to be as successful as the campaign behind it to drive app use.

When Beacons Go Right

Beacons allow that kind of joined up, tailored and personalized ads on your mobile as you walk around a store. It's like adding a digital layer onto your shopping experience.

What does this layer look like? At it's most simple, when you walk into a store or venue using beacon technology your phone would vibrate and you'd see a message on your screen that welcomes you to the store, perhaps with a discount or offer.

The real value in beacons is in four areas: footfall tracking, personalised offers, storytelling in store, and multi-channel eCRM.

– Footfall tracking
Beacons can track mobiles as they move around a building, meaning you can see hour-by-hour live footfall statistics across your estate as moves move from department to department within your store or venue. This data can be used to streamline operations and staffing as well as plan offers.

– Personalized loyalty offers
Shoppers can be segmented by demographics, previous online purchase behaviour, or even heavy app users, and personalized, highly targeted offers can be delivered in store. Messages can be sent to lapsed returning visitors or to people on, say, their third visit.

If a store uses several beacons, you can set to trigger a message to be sent when someone is near the category they are most interested in. For example, all shoppers who abandoned an online cart can be sent a promotion to their mobile for the same item when they are close by the store.

– Storytelling in store
Because messages are triggered by proximity to the beacons and require no action from the shopper, notifications can be used to tell a story around a store.

Imagine walking into a grocery store and receiving a welcome message with a promotion on steak and wine. Then, as you pass fresh food, you're sent menu suggestions with *buy together* offers.

Because the technology is accurate up to one metre, users could even ask for directions to a product location and be shown where to go. The key is to make sure that offers are used cautiously and to avoid spamming the user.

Messages can be time-delayed too, so you can trigger a *Can we help you?* message 10 minutes after someone enters a fashion store, inviting them to discover more about products on their phone, or to visit customer services or a personal shopper.

– Multi-channel eCRM
Using beacons alongside CRM software, you can use shopper data to send targeted messages by push notification or email that offers related products or triggered campaigns.

For example, beacons can identify people sitting in a cinema audience who have downloaded the cinema app and then follow up by email with communications related to the ads they watched before the movie.

How Do We Make Beacons Work?

Beacons promise a great deal, but also have two key shopper barriers to entry: 1) The shopper must have previously downloaded the app and 2) They must have Bluetooth on when they shop. Which is why that successful beacon campaigns always start with a robust app awareness and download strategy and end with an awareness campaign at store for shoppers to turn on their Bluetooth to access exclusive offers and a digital shopping experience. In the case of the Regent Street app, both of these elements seem to be missing.

Get these elements right, such as in the Swan Centre in Eastleigh, and as you walk in the shopping centre doors, you're reminded about the app and to have Bluetooth on, and are instantly rewarded with points to redeem in various stores as well as a free cup of coffee.

Here's how to implement beacons for success:

1. Gather shopper insight, contextual shopper behaviour and discover the media landscape. How are your shoppers shopping, and how much do they use smartphone apps? While there are hurdles to beacon use, the shopper is willing to trial them. According to a survey by eDigitalResearch, 45% of UK shoppers would be *very willing* or *somewhat willing* for retailers to send messages to their smartphone, and 78% of those would be willing for retailers to use this data if it meant more personalised messages for them.

2. Plan a test-and-learn campaign. What's the campaign's purpose? To enhance an experience – e.g. in a fashion store or at an entertainment venue? To deliver targeted offers and promotions, or instant rewards? To offer direction and customer service?

3. Identify key retail locations, venues or OOH sites. Define heavy mobile users or relevant segments we might aim to target first.

4. Integrate Bluetooth capability into your existing app, or plan your app build. Suppliers may want to partner to use a retailer's existing app.

5. Create a marketing campaign to encourage target shoppers to download the app.

6. Plan the location of the beacon, the trigger mechanism – e.g. distance, time-delay, and plan the messages, message frequency and relevance. Consider if messaging is required in store to remind users to turn on their phone's Bluetooth or to download the app.

7. Check: Is the beacon strategy full integrated (or has the potential to be in future) into an eCRM strategy?

8. Analyse campaign for insights and to consider extending the trial reach and scope.

Tracking Shoppers In Store Without Freaking Them Out

The last few years, there's been an increasing interest in talking to shoppers one on one. On a website, you can use cookies to store information about an individual to serve them content and offers specific to them. Cookies are non-intrusive and most of the time we don't notice that content is served up especially for us. It just feels like a good experience.

Translate the need for a *single consumer view* to the physical retail stores and it's easy for things to get messy.

One company recently got in touch with me to demonstrate its totem that can serve personalised content on its screen. You approach it, and it displays a personal message for you, including your name and a photo of you.

"Isn't it great!" the enthusiastic new businessperson said. "No, I think it's awful," was my reply. I don't know about you, but seeing my name and photo grabbed from my Facebook profile displayed in public on a giant screen would freak me out. It would feel like an invasion of my privacy. I'd worry what other content it was going to show me. Was it going to reveal my browsing history, giving away to my wife what I've bought her for her birthday, or worse, displaying to the world my purchase of a whole host of 50 *Shades of Grey* sex kit?

To market to individuals, you first need good data of what people are doing inside your retail store. There are two ways to get this without freaking out your customers that give you online analytics for the real world. You can follow shoppers and visitors in store to discover dwell time, loyalty and detailed real-time shopping habits.

While footfall tracking isn't new, what these new technologies makes possible is just really impressive from an operations or a marketing standpoint.

Would it be useful to know exactly when each store or venue in your estate was busiest? Would it be useful to which in-store hours were most profitable? Would you like to save costs on staffing by getting staffing levels to precisely match the number of customers in each store? Would you like to know how customers move around a store or venue in real time? Would you be interested to know whether men or women buy more at different hours, and be able to track different audience segments around a store and understand their behaviour – all the time and in every store?

Enter Wi-Fi, which can be set up to measure the number of people in-store and track their dwell time. Retailers can plan staffing levels around when they're most busy, or make sure stores are stocked and presented well before the busiest times.

Wi-Fi also enables retailers to track footfall both inside the location and nearby. From this they can work out the level of passing traffic and how that converts into either an in-store or in-venue visit. Once they've established a baseline for the average *street to store conversion*, they can then measure the impact of a new window display or marketing campaign.

Just like a house address, or a computer IP address, every smartphone has a unique address called a Mac code. If you've ever swapped your home broadband supplier, you'll have heard of Mac codes, because Wi-Fi routers have them too and you had to find out your Mac code to move your broadband.

Here's the clever bit… your phone is always broadcasting its Mac code to any nearby Wi-Fi routers. It does this whether you have Wi-Fi on or not. And it's this feature that allows a special way to monitor footfall with a store or venue.

As a person approaches the venue or store that's using Wi-Fi footfall tracking, the Wi-Fi router in store will register their smartphone. The moment the person walks through the venue or store doors, the technology will register the person as a shopper or visitor.

As you can set up the technology to recognize the perimeter of the store or venue, you can receive hour-by-hour statistics of the number of people in the store, and how long they stay in store – the dwell time. Use the technology for a few weeks and it allows you to consider operational efficiencies across your store and venue estate, as well as to see almost instantly how busy your estate is from head office on any given day or any given hour. Want to know if your stores are busier this Saturday than last Saturday? You got it. Want to know which time of day is busiest for passing trade outside your venue? You got it.

This means that you can plan your staffing levels around when the store or venue is most busy, or make sure stores are stocked and presented well before the busiest times. These means that staff savings and efficiencies can be achieved.

And because the system can be linked to a growing number of EPOS systems, in-store footfall peaks and troughs can be compared to in-store sales peaks and troughs. Imagine discovering that the peak time for in store footfall is 4pm, but that the second biggest footfall peak at 11am results much higher average purchase sales.
Consider how that might affect your staffing and store readiness. You might operate a skeleton staff till the store begins to get busy at 10am, make sure the most expensive lines were merchandised well by 11am and ensure your best sales staff were on the floor by then. By 4am, you'd have made lower priced items more prominent with bargains and impulse purchases prominent and remind staff to offer upgrades and upsells at till.

There are also intriguing marketing insights that this new technology can give us. Because we can track both the footfall inside the store or venue and the footfall within a radius outside of store or venue, we can calibrate these results to help us find out the amount of passing traffic that then converts to an in-store or in-venue visit. Once you have established a baseline for your average *street to store conversion*, you can then measure the effect of a new window display or marketing campaign – do store conversations increase or decrease based on the new windows?

Mobile Footfall Tracking Using Beacons

Beacons are small electronic devices less than half the size of a phone, which can be attached anywhere – a wall, fixture, doorway or shelf edge.

They can track smartphones and tell you down to the metre how far away it is from the beacon. However, compared to Wi-Fi tracking, tracking using beacons requires that the shopper or visitor has previously opted in to the use of the devices, which means there are less privacy concerns as well as enhanced trackability. The downside is that only a percentage of visitors or shopper will have opted in.

This kind of tracking is permission-based, which there has to be a good reason for the shopper or visitor to allow us to know where they are when they enter the store or venue. That reason is the ability to access valuable offers, discounts and further information on products or services.

The shopper or visitor has to get access to these offers by downloading an app. This could be encouraged months or years before, or as they enter the store or venue. The app prompts them to allow *location services*, and in-store or in-venue signs reminds them to turn on their Bluetooth connection. This allows them to access better offers and services than those visitors and shoppers not using the app.

Now we have permission to access the shopper's or visitor's location information, we can track them around the venue. The power of user beacons is that we can track people minute-by-minute, metre-by-metre. We can place several beacons in a department of the store or each area of the venue and track how a customer moves around. In the same way that Google Analytics shows you how people click from page to page around a website, we can look at how people move around a physical location.

Because the system is permission-based, we can track smartphone users' dwell time as well as be able to segment shoppers or visitors, so we can see how first time visitors behave, or those who shop twice a week or more, for example.

We can also look at shoppers' or visitors' behaviour based on other data too that was collected at the point the app was downloaded and used. Let's say you collected the users' email addresses when they logged into the app. You'd now be able to segment shoppers or visitors by those who open your emails frequently or rarely and using the footfall tracking, be able to see if those more engaged with the brand behave differently in store. Imagine if you'd asked for postcode data when they logged into the app, you could see how frequently different geographical segments visit the store or venue.

And because you're using beacon technology, we can do so much more than footfall tracking, such as sending offers and customer service messages direct to people's smartphones as they walk around. Messages can be triggered by specific beacons, so you can send visitors to a leisure venue a welcome message, or deliver sophisticated offers, such as a coupon with a great discount to first-time shoppers to a store, but one that expires in ten minutes.

Who Is Tracking Shoppers?

An increasing number of retailers... Department store Nordstrom has run a trial Wi-Fi mobile footfall tracking across specific departments of 17 of its stores. Home Depot have trialled it too. Because of concerns around shopper reactions to the use of this technology, many companies who have trailed Wi-Fi footfall tracking have been unwilling to discuss it publically. Beacon-based technology has been trialled by Macy's and Duane Reade in the US and Eat and Coca Cola in the UK. Though these companies have primarily talked about the messaging capability of beacons and Bluetooth, the ability to measure footfall in store is undoubtedly a key operational and marketing benefit to these trials.

Okay, I'm interested. What now?

Because the technology is relatively new, the emerging high growth start-up companies in this area are adding new features and uses month by month. Some key areas to focus mobile footfall tracking trials on are:

• Diagnose poor performing sales and time in store. Placing mobile footfall technology in store or in venues allows fast comparisons of footfall and dwell time across an estate. Linking these systems to EPOS means we can see which stores are the most and least engaging and make the least and most sales and identify how the high engagement stores drives footfall and sales. Once staff training has been implemented into poor performing stores, the effectiveness can be measured by any uplift in dwell time and sales.

• Identify sales and product opportunities. By measuring footfall outside the store window, we can identify the busiest times of the day and week and identify future products and services to offer to drive revenue. For example, if you notice high footfall in front of a QSR store at breakfast time, is there an opportunity to start serving breakfast?

• Tracking return visitors and loyalty; using footfall tracking to compare the behaviour of first-time visitors and shoppers and frequent visitors; finding which venues in your estate have high loyalty and which don't. This insight allows us to pinpoint training and local marketing campaigns to increase loyalty across the estate.

• Testing national and local campaign effectiveness on store visits. Let's say you run a new ATL or BTL campaign and sales are not what you hoped across all of the estate. Perhaps sales are flat in some stores where you've used direct mail to support awareness of the campaign and drive people to the stores. By developing a new local marketing campaign to those stores, we can then compare footfall before and after running the new supporting campaign, which leads us to create more efficient campaigns in the future.

• Following up with your highest value customers. Once you've identified who your frequent visitors are with the highest dwell times, we can develop and eCRM strategy to reward them and encourage loyalty and advocacy.

Whichever uses of mobile footfall technology are most promising to your brand, the best approach is to run a two to four week trial in a single store. The most common response of clients to a mobile footfall tracking trial is amazement at the power of the technology, which often results in discussions on how to roll out across an estate and identify clearly which features and functionality are to be introduced in phases.

Getting Personal With Messaging

So now we've got our data on what people are doing in our stores. Is it now time to install that 6-sheet that calls out the shoppers' names and interest in sex dungeon equipment? Probably not.

There are plenty of options to deliver personalised messages with screens available with facial recognition technology, or beacons built in to recognise individual app users. But I suggest staying clear of this kind of tech for now, or at least limiting its use.

As consumers, we're used to the concept of sharing our data to get a better customer experience or service. Tesco's Clubcard and Facebook are great examples where we don't even consider the issue of data privacy – we just enjoy the benefits that these services bring.

However, Facebook is confined to the privacy of a screen we control, and while Tesco sends us personalised offers in our letterbox based on previous purchases, it stops there on broadcasting our preferences.

Here's my golden rule: Never display personal public information on a public screen.

While we could have a shelf barker saying, *Hey Fred, you previously bought Omega 3 fish fingers, here's £1 off your next purchase*, we should not do it.

My advice is to use data not to call out the fact that you have access to single consumer view data. Do not use a person's name or photo on a screen in a public place.

But what you could do is use the data you have to anonymously segment your shoppers. You could tailor your screen messages so that the store experience just feels more right for each shopper.

There are some options for how to do this:

1. Target messaging by sex
Some screens use facial recognition to determine how many male and female faces are in the vicinity. You could then change the messaging based on the makeup of the audience. To use a stereotyped example, a grocer could run signage about summer BBQs, and switch messages from grilled chicken, salads and white wine to target female shoppers, then swap the message to talk more about burgers and beer.

Personally, I'm not keen on this idea. One, because my wife is slapping me right now for being so sexist, and two, because I can't imagine many cases where an audience might swing from majority male to majority female and back again to make this kind of targeted messaging effective.

2. Use data that doesn't relate to people, but does change shopper behaviour
The best example of this is changing screen messaging based on weather conditions. On a warm summer's day, swap the messaging in a coffee shop to ice lattes. On a cooler day, switch back to hot coffees.

You've not used any shopper data, but you can use footfall tracking on till receipts to see how your messaging is affecting sales in real time and to which customer segments, allowing you to adjust your in store marketing and to follow up with more personalised eCRM messages later.

3. Make messages targeted, not personalised
Having a digital shelf barker that says, *Hey Fred, you previously bought Omega 3 fish fingers, here's £1 off your next purchase* is too personal, but that doesn't mean that you can't use the data to deliver a similar message. If you know Fred is in front of the screen, you could show this message: *Omega 3 fish fingers: £1 off your purchase.* There's a very good chance Fred won't even know that message is speaking to him. But there's also a very good chance that by delivering the message for him, you'll get more sales.

If that still feels a little bit too stalker-ish, you could show three rotating messages – one or two which are based on previous purchase history and one or two that's based on a lookalike algorithm. If Fred is 35 to 45 years old and has kids and you know his segment buys more chicken nuggets, then you could deliver a chicken nuggets message in the hope that Fred is typical of the segment, alongside those messages meant just for him.

So No *Minority Report* Yet Then?

The same rules apply to beacon messaging too. The rule applies to any message that is to be delivered in a public place. Emails, direct mail – personalise the hell out of them. Just don't do it on screens.

Remember the screen in *Minority Report* where Tom Cruise walks through the shopping mall and the advertising billboards call out to him with personalised messages? Maybe people will become used to the concept in a few years, and us marketers start to move into that type of personalisation.

But maybe consumers won't ever want that. It's better to err on the side of caution and maintain a trusted relationship with your shoppers, than to risk that trust and have your customer feel that their data has been used in a creepy way to manipulate them.

The rule is simple: don't be a douche. If ever you think your targeting is particularly clever, just check in and ask yourself, "Is it also douchy?"

Step 3 Key Points:
Hacking The In-Store Experience

• Three in four millennials (78%) would choose to spend money on an experience or event over buying something desirable [source: Harris Associates, 2015]. Retailers need to engage millennials with experiences or become obsolete.

• One in three UK shoppers (34%) want a better in-store experience, while 1 in 5 (18%) think that the shopping experience on the High Street is getting worse (rising to 21% of 25- to 34-year-olds [source: State of Retail 2016, Live & Breathe, 2016].

• Digital needs to be employed (appropriately, and alongside more traditional methods) to enhance and innovate the customer experience.

• High Streets and shopping centres used to do people where people went shopping because they offered convenience, ease of shop and a wide range. When e-commerce handles these factors well, what is the role of physical retail stores? It's the store experience.

• One of the biggest challenges with digital signage and other technology in store is that screens still don't come cheap. But there are ways to bring aspects of digital in store, or items that do the same job as big screens – grab attention – at a fraction of the cost.

• Digital for hygiene. Digital technology can play a key role in the customer experience through enhancing hygiene factors such as ease of use, speed of delivery, range and cost.

• There are huge opportunities to use mobile in store to gather insight and drives sales. Consider mobile apps, digital coupons, mobile payments and beacon messaging. But don't be a douche and freak customers out with creepy messages that use too much data.

Jobs To Be Done:

- Identify which business lens is the best fit to focus your digital investment: 1) Cost efficiencies and revenue generation; 2) Marketing efficiency; 3) Brand experience.

- Audit the technology in your retail estate and compare with your direct competitors. What are you using technology for? Where are you making the best use of technology? What can you learn from your competitors?

Step 4:

Jail-Breaking E-Commerce: Freeing Sales From Its Desktop Prison

Now that e-commerce is 20+ years old, it's easy to forget how far we've come. I remember being an early user of Amazon and eBay, and signing up to PayPal when it arrived in the UK, and noticing the worried looks of my friends and family who believed that if you put your credit card details in a web page, someone would steal your details and empty your bank account.

The internet in the late 90s and early 00s wasn't seen as a place that was trusted, or where brands you trusted did commerce. At best it was a place where brands had a corporate website.

Now, the biggest concern about e-commerce is not security of payments, but how quick and easy it is to buy something. If the design of an e-commerce shop is confusing, we hit the back button and go elsewhere. If the checkout process is complicated, we'll give up. Is shipping is costly or takes weeks, we're out of there. Amazon and PayPal offer us one-button checkouts, ASOS offers free delivery, and Amazon offers 1-hour delivery in an increasing number of UK cities.

Shopping used to help us buy what we need. Now we can get what we want and get it now.

See it. Buy it. Job done.

The twin growth engines of e-commerce – ease of shop and convenience – mean that we want to be able to buy something the moment the urge takes us. As brands and retailers looking to satisfy that urge, we need to help e-commerce break out of its desktop prison. People want to buy at the touch of a button. They want to buy any time, any place, on any device, on any touchpoint.

There are two steps to help e-commerce free itself from the desktop prison:

1. Embrace M-commerce. It's a silly word, but it does embrace the idea that commerce happens on mobile devices with increasing frequency. PCs are still a huge sales channel. iPads are used for browsing more often than sales. And smartphones are the home of e-commerce.

Whether your shoppers want a mobile-optimised website or a mobile app, or both, buying stuff on mobiles needs to be incredibly easy. Every click and tap and character that needs to be typed in should be seen as a barrier to purchase. Dominos Pizza understand this need for easy of shop, and has been developing ways of removing virtually all friction to purchase as possible.

One idea is to give their most loyal customers a button that can sit on the coffee table. It connects by Bluetooth to your mobile, and when you press the button it orders your favourite pizza for delivery and charges your bank. One press is all it needs.
The other innovation Dominos has been testing is the ability to set up its app, so that when you tap the app icon to open it on your phone, your favourite pizza is ordered. If you opened the app but didn't want or order a pizza there and then, you have 10 seconds to cancel your order.

While both of these innovations take ease of shop to the extreme, they illustrate the direction that e-commerce is heading in: ease of shop and convenience rules.

2. Embrace Distributed E-Commerce. Again, it's a bit of a crap name, but the concept behind it is a powerful one. Distributed e-commerce is a marketing principle that suggests that any communications touchpoint can also becomes a sales touchpoint. Your digital media can drive awareness, your Facebook posts can engage and your website can tell your product or retail story, but what they can also do is drive immediate sales.

For FMCG brands, you do this by using add to cart technology. You add a button or a web link to those digital ads or website that allows your audience to add your product to the shopping cart of their favourite online grocer. They can then go on to complete their order straight away or save it in the cart until they are ready to do a bigger shop. The same principle can be followed for retailers – all digital touchpoints can provide a link or a button to drive people to an e-commerce cart there and then. To make this process as easy as possible, you can even add products to a cart from an online ad without ever leaving the page you're on.

To find out more about how this *add to cart* technology works to create a distributed e-commerce strategy, check out the likes of Adimo, Shopwyre and Dotter.

Plotting A Path To Purchase In A ROPO World

Research online, purchase offline (ROPO) is a concept that's been with us for a while now, but it doesn't always affect how campaigns are briefed or media is booked as much as it should. For example, channels such as social media are resource intensive but don't always return as high a multiplier on investment as other channels.

With this in mind, the Live & Breathe State of Retail survey 2016 asked its shopper panel how they planned a purchase in three specific categories: clothing, entertaining and TV buying. It found that the strongest ROPO journey was for TV buying, with 60% researching online several times before buying. Only 32% of those then completed a purchase online with 36% of people going into a physical store to buy. Twenty-four per cent of respondents said they went in store several times before they bought.

The survey asked which behaviours people would do if they were cooking a special meal. The results were a landslide: 61% go in store to buy. The next closest result was *research online several times* at 21%. Only 12% said they would buy online, perhaps indicating that the limitations of grocery shopping e-commerce sites are not enabling shoppers to be inspired for food shopping beyond the everyday purchases. One side note: approximately one-third of those who wrote additional comments against this question said they did not cook.

Buying new clothes is the most multi-channel experience, according to the survey respondents.

Fifty-eight per cent go in store to buy clothes, while 40% buy online. One in four of us research online several times before making a purchase, slightly higher than the 23% of us who go into a physical store several times before we buy.

To understand how to make the most of your e-commerce site/app, we need to build a ROPO picture of the world for your products. This ROPO understanding of the path to purchase will tell you how to make the most of paid, owned and earned media. It will also help you join up the e-commerce and physical retail parts of your organisation: If you know where sales ultimately take place, it will help define the role of each channel. Perhaps e-commerce is not just a sales channel for your business, but also a supporting channel to drive physical store sales. And vice versa.

Click & Collect Beats Mobile And Tablets For Tech Innovation

According to Live & Breathe's State of Retail survey, seven times more people say online shopping is getting better because of more Click & Collect (28%) than say it is getting worse because of poor or no Click & Collect (4%).

When asked, *Which one technology changed the way you shopped in 2015?*, Click & Collect was the top answer (19%), beating mobile phones, tablets and smart watches. For those who have not already fully integrated Click & Collect into their supply chain and offer to shoppers, now is the time to make that a priority.

Convenience Beats Range Online

Half of shoppers (50%) say that online shopping is getting more convenient in the Live & Breathe State Of Retail survey. When asked, *If you had to shop online or on the High Street for the rest of your life, which would you choose?*, 55% of people chose online.

Online shopping covers off the hygiene factors really well. Convenience is the No.1 rated improvement in the channel, followed closely by more choice/greater selection (47%) and more value (45%).

There's evidence that UK shoppers are happy to stick with High Street brands online when these hygiene factors are met. Thirty-five per cent of people cited more brands going online as something they liked, and more than one in four (28%) said more retailers with Click & Collect was an improvement. However, only 10% of people said customer service was getting better, and 11% said it was getting worse.

Scores for *what's getting worse* about online shopping are the lowest in the survey, much lower than scores for the High Street or shopping centres. A huge 68% selected none of the options for areas that needed improving. The No.1 answer in this area was that 16% of people would like even more choice/greater selection.

Perhaps this feedback is most relevant to traditional retailers moving into e-commerce and specialist stores, where perhaps logistics or number of brands stocked limits the range available.

Appetite For One-Hour Delivery Driven By Same-Day Delivery Success

Next, the Live & Breathe survey asked which aspects of delivery besides Click & Collect would influence shoppers to order online more. Sixty-nine per cent say they would shop more online if free delivery was included. Forty-nine per cent of shoppers said that same-day delivery would make them more likely to increase their number of shops.

Surprisingly, 43% said that one-hour delivery would make them buy more online, despite only a small number of people having tried the service through Amazon Prime Now in London and Birmingham.

Drone deliveries would only prompt more shops in 13% of people, while self-driving cars would interest 10% of shoppers, so beyond PR stunts the appetite for novel delivery methods is still yet to capture the public's imagination.

While Click & Collect can sometimes be implemented into operations with little cost, home delivery can make some basket spends unprofitable. But shoppers' expectations are being shaped by next-day, same-day and one-hour delivery, so the challenge for the future is to satisfy shopper expectations with delivery options, within acceptable profit margins.

The New E-Commerce Categories

With almost one in ten (9%) of UK shoppers buying online for the first time in 2015, there's plenty of growth in e-commerce.

Even categories that have been sold online for 20 years still show room for growth with 56% of survey respondents having shopped online for clothing last year, 51% for books and 38% for DVDs [source: Live & Breathe State of Retail 2016].

Thirty-two per cent of shoppers say they bought groceries online in 2015, but only one in four are buying white goods online (27%) and furniture stands at 13%. This might indicate that for some categories, especially where larger purchases are made, being able to touch and feel products and talk to a member of staff in person is important, and online sites such as AO.com need to find ways to overcome these barriers to purchase.

The Live & Breathe survey data indicates a sweet spot for online shopping growth: where decisions are relatively simple, speed and convenience are a necessity, and the sector has few traditional players aiming to disrupt it with technology. This sweet spot includes takeaway delivery, vegetable and grocery box delivery, and recipe kit boxes.

Nineteen per cent of people ordered takeaways online in 2015. Given that the takeaway sector is a sizeable existing market, and that buying takeaways instead of cooking is thoroughly embedded in our shopping behaviour, it's perhaps surprising that the ease and speed of online ordering has not led more of us to buy takeaways online.

Ongoing marketing pushes by the likes of Just Eat, Deliveroo and Hungry House, alongside innovations such as Domino's at-home button (one press and your favourite pizza is ordered for delivery) should see impressive growth in 2016. The challenge for this sector is how to handle the endless choice the shopper has – which cuisine, restaurant and dish do I choose?

Vegetable box providers such as Abel & Cole may have been around for a long time, but with Amazon Pantry and Amazon Fresh entering the UK market, the concept of weekly, next day or same-day delivery of fresh foods and store cupboard essentials is set to make a real impact in 2016. While 7% used any kind of Click & Collect for the first time ever last year, 8% ordered vegetable and food boxes in 2015, indicating there's plenty of room for growth.

The challenge for this sector depends on whether to have deep pockets or not so deep pockets. For Amazon, the challenge is to see if it can change our shopping habits from supermarket shopping to online delivery of food with Amazon. For Abel & Cole and others like it, the challenge is how to compete with the cash reserves, logistics and marketing clout of Amazon entering this market.

Traditional retailers moving into this space need to have a value proposition that matches Amazon's and/or a brand proposition that sets them apart from Amazon. The newest entrant to the online retail market that we asked our shopper panel about was recipe kit boxes, such as Hello Fresh or Gousto. Only 6% of UK shoppers have tried a service like this, which might indicate that greater awareness of these services is needed, or that these services need to make their offering more flexible or to have more clarity around whether convenience or inspiration is more important to the shopper.

The Long Tail

Named by *Wired* magazine US editor Chris Anderson, the long tail describes online sales beyond the most popular SKUs. The basics of the long tail concept is that there are four different kinds of product sales:

1. Breakout hits, e.g. a two-litre bottle of Coca Cola

2. Very popular core products, e.g. Heinz Spaghetti Hoops

3. Niche products with good sales, e.g. Vitamin Water; energy bars; soya milk

4. A long tail of products, with low sales of each SKU, e.g. ironing water; Booja Booja ice cream; Fentiman's Cream Soda

Eighty per cent of sales in a large format supermarket will come from 1 and 2 perhaps that percentage is even higher in smaller, local stores.

The problem with physical stores is that while 20% of sales volume is made up by categories 3. and 4., shelf space is limited, so every new product demanding shelf space will mean another product will have its listings cut or removed. For most shoppers, they'll never notice a product they never considered before suddenly missing from the shelf, but to a small number of shoppers, that now-missing SKU might have been one of their favourite buys.

How does e-commerce and online help solve this problem? Because shelf space online is infinite. In theory, you could list every product ever produced and give shoppers the ultimate experience in consumer choice.

Of course, the reality is that limitless shelf space isn't necessary really limitless. As we explored above, the number of products made available becomes limited by shoppers' attention span. They don't actually want to browse every product ever made. They trust their supermarket to make a curated choice for them, so much so that we don't ever stop to consider that retailers are making this curation for us.

But you do want to maximize the increasing returns of adding extra SKUs, because the long tail theory says that even the occasional purchase of a single SKU, when multiplied by thousands and thousands of SKUs, adds up to good revenue. Amazon learned this and built their business on the long tail, stocking everything you might possibly want to buy.

Yes, shelf space is limited by attention, but this means that product selection is no longer limited by physical space, but by how those products are ordered in an online store so that relevant and interesting long tail SKUs are surfaced to the right shoppers.

We'll explore the implications that the long tail has for online store design in Step 4.

An understanding of the long tail also affects how we consider online and in store sales. We already know that not all products are equal: Coke and Birds Eye are more valuable brands than Fentiman's Cola and Young's because of the brand equity and the volume of sales that each brand drives. As we mentioned before, these brands represent parts 1 and 2 On the long tail distribution curve: Breakout Hits and Very Popular Core Products.

But what about segments 3. and 4:

3. Niche products with good sales, e.g. Vitamin Water; energy bars; soya milk

4. A long tail of products, with low sales of each SKU, e.g. ironing water; Booja Booja ice cream; Fentiman's Cream Soda

These areas of the curve can be given more time, more space and more attention to fulfil their sales potential in an e-commerce store compared with a brick and mortar one because space is less of a limitation, meaning that the affect on a Breakout Hit of showing an extra SKU for a niche product are tiny.

Sure, I know we talked about too much choice being a bad thing and cannibalising sales, but giving space to 3 and 4 as well as 1 and 2 is a design problem to be solved, so that choice blindness does not set in? If products are grouped right and presented correctly to those who are interested in them, the issue of too much choice can be dwarfed by the extra sales associated with sales of niche products along the long tail.

The key takeaway from thinking about long tail economics is that we can assess ROI and success of a product portfolio for each segment. If we're considering stocking a new SKU, we can identify if we think it fits into segment 1, 2, 3 or 4, which would give us an expectation of sales volume, niche interest and how and where we place the product listing on the website. By thinking this way, we can maximize long tail sales and add up to 20% more sales to our online store.

CX + UX

In Step 3: Hacking The In-Store Experience, we discussed the importance of the customer experience (CX). We said that the future of physical retail relies on a greater attention to designing the stores with the customer in mind, so they weren't just buying; they were able to have an enjoyable experience of our brand.

The in-store CX is what differentiates physical retail from online retail. Personal service and being able to touch and experience products is key, as is the enjoyment of shopping with friends and family in a great environment.

Leading retailers (and those that are thriving on the High Street in five years' time) will focus on changing the retail experience, from store layouts that allow people to experience more than consume, to store formats such as small format stores in city centres that meet people's needs better.

Shoppers want retailers to focus on a great experience because it's not delivering at the moment.

But when it comes to online experience (e-commerce experiences), user experience (UX) often does a poor job of mimicking personal service online. There are three main ways that personal experiences are delivered in e-commerce stores:

1. Personalised shelves and content
We track the shopper's browsing behaviour in an app or website, and based on what they look at, we show them more things they might like. Amazon's *People Who Bought X, Also Bought...* is the obvious example. You can use code to change your website content on the fly so that what's shown in the store depends on who's viewing it. Personalised offers can be delivered on screen without the shopper even knowing they are seeing deals created just for them.

2. Online chat
Customer service in person can't be beat. Or can it? While it's easier to build rapport and grow to like someone in person, when it comes to engaging with customer service people in retailers, building a rapport isn't usually what we're thinking. We need help finding something. Or advice. And online chat agents can do that as well (or sometimes better) than in-store staff. In-store staff might have a number of jobs to do, from managing stock to manning the tills to customer service.

When you hire teams for online support, you can focus on making them the absolute best at handling queries as efficiently and as helpfully as possible. And many more companies are embracing the idea that e-commerce or websites need to be able to hold a two-way conversation, rather than just display products. If you ask an ASOS online customer service person what colour shirt would suit you best, they'll help you out. Wine.com is increasing its online staff to be available 24 hours to answer customers' queries about quality wines for the sophisticated (and busy) wine connoisseur.

3. Personalised products

Have you ever shopped at Vistaprint, the online printing company? Once you upload a design and go to check out, you're then shown a range of other products featuring your design. If you typed in your name and company name to create some business cards, you're shown how your company details look on headed paper, sticky labels, company T-shirts etc.

This is a clear example of aiming to drive more sales from showing products that only have value to you, the current shopper. Increasingly, brands and retailers are applying personalisation to their offering. The car dealer who upsells metallic paint has always known the value of personalised products. Now with the current trend in print-on-demand FMCG brands, personalisation is coming to the fore, from personalised Nutella jars to bottles of Famous Grouse with a special message printed on the label for my dad on Father's Day.

Where personalisation will soon become disruptive to both e-commerce and physical retailers in the next few years is with the ability to 3D print products. 3D printing means that my personal tastes can influence the final product. I can even design something myself and have it printed. This has been an area that T-shirt printers have encouraged for a long time. But as 3D printers become cheaper and are able to print in multiple materials to a high standard and low cost, there will come a point when some people will be okay with buying the standard Ikea sofa, while others will want to pick a crowd-designed product or design one themselves.

Whichever combination of the above your team uses to create a better user experience of your e-commerce offering, we have to bear in mind that UX stands for user experience and not brand experience. There might be a certain kind of brand experience we want people to have when using our e-commerce channels, but the key to success is to tailor the UX to the shopper's current mind-set. Are they on a mission to buy quickly, or do they want to be inspired? How can we design our online experiences to find out what the user wants and then give them the best experience?

Distributed E-commerce

To truly free online sales from its desktop prison, we have to free ourselves from the idea that online sales need to happen at an e-commerce website at all. In the mobile world, e-commerce could happen anywhere.

The term for this is distributed e-commerce. If you've seen online ads with an *add to cart* button, you've already seen distributed e-commerce in action.

On the next page is an example of an online ad for Old Spice that's been turned into a checkout by technology company – and distributed e-commerce pioneer – Adimo.

You see the ad as you're browsing the internet, and perhaps you click the *add to basket* button. Without taking you away from the website you're browsing, the creative of the ad changes, asking you to select an online retailer to buy from.

You choose your retailer, then the content of the ad changes again to give you a choice of product.

If you're still logged into your retailer account, when you click the *add* button, your item is added to the basket. You can leave it there to check out later when you're doing a bigger shop, or you can click to check out, which will then – and only then – open up a new web page to check out.

If you're not currently logged into your retailer account, you can login from the same ad.

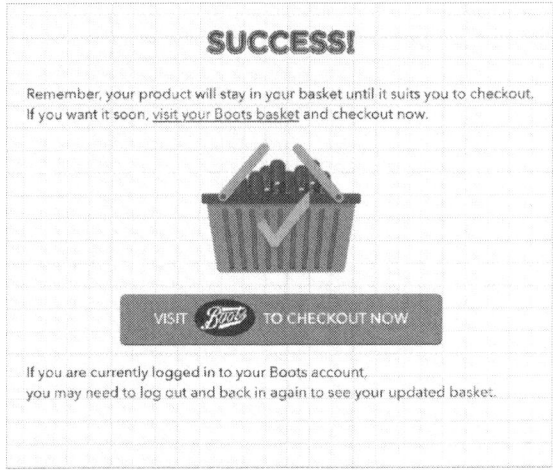

Viv Craske   157

This distributed e-commerce innovation has a number of advantages:

• You can turn your marketing assets into checkouts – drive direct response e-commerce sales from all digital comms. You can drive sales from your online ads, your social media posts and ads, your brand site or competition micro-site.

• You can drive impulse purchases. If someone is really interested in your ad, rather than hoping they'll remember you next time they're shopping, you can turn that interest into an action immediately.

• Even if people only add the product to their online shopping cart and don't go on to buy it shortly afterwards, by getting the shopper to select your product and click it, you're increasing their purchase consideration of the brand.

• Adding *add to cart* buttons to your online media can increase your awareness and engagement metrics. When you use *add to cart* buttons with your YouTube videos, for example, time spent viewing the video increases by an average of 35 seconds, as people browse your product range.

• *Add to cart* buttons drive engagement, causing cost per engagement for paid media campaigns I've seen decrease by 75% on average.

• You can get granular engagement and sales data. Because this technology can be integrated across many channels, you get to find out which ads drive interest in which products driving logins to which retailers.

• You can sell the range. An online ad may be too small to showcase an entire product range or category. However, when people click the *add to basket* button and are invited to explore the range, we get to drive awareness and purchase intent of a lot more than one or two products.

• It's easy and convenient for shoppers. They can buy from within a banner ad, never needing to leave the webpage they are on.

• It's easy to scale. With dozens of retailer integrations, across Europe or the world, leading tech companies like Adimo can scale across European or global campaigns easily.

Driving Physical Store Sales With Digital Coupons

The number one challenge with digital marketing used to be that it was hard to attribute the vale of digital media spend to sales uplift. You'd spend money on online banners and social media posts and a sequence of emails, but you'd never know what impact those channels had in the marketing mix when it actually came to tracking sales.

Sure, you could point to reach or impressions of the digital marketing channels, but how did we know if all that effort actually translated into sales?

(In many ways, this is an unfair comparison digital channels have always had to contend with. For a large number of FMCG and retailer campaigns, the specific value of a TV ad in isolation, or a radio ad, or a print ad is not measured. And even if it is, it can't be measured precisely.)

But now with the increase in digital couponing solutions, we finally have the Holy Grail – the ability to track digital comms from eyeballs through to precise sales numbers.

Digital Coupons For Retailers

Here's how it works.

If you are a retailer...

• Companies such as Eagle Eye have a system that allows us to create coupons with unique codes.

• We could mention a coupon in paid online media, email, web, social etc., lead people to a simple web opt-in page and deliver the coupon to the shopper by email.

• Coupons could be mentioned in printed materials, with either a call to action to the opt-in web page, or with a unique printed code.

• The coupon is redeemed in store when the shopper shows the coupon in an email – or as a screen grab – on a mobile phone, or showing a printed coupon.

• When the coupon is redeemed in store (or online), the code is verified by the back-end system and marked as redeemed.

• Data of the redemption can be passed to our retailer's CRM system to add to their contact record the fact that they have recently used a coupon.

Notes:
1. Companies like Eagle Eye will charge you a monthly license fee to use its system, as well as a cost per coupon issuance and cost per redemption.
2. You may need to upgrade your EPOS system and/or hardware to make digital couponing work for you.

The joy of digital couponing is being able to create an end-to-end digital campaign that is completely trackable. You can track the number of clicks on the media you use to drive awareness, through to number of coupons issued to number redeemed. And you can use that data to make increasingly efficient digital sales-driving campaigns, all the while updating your CRM database, to create segments of shoppers who have responded to offers in the past.

If you're as excited as me about end-to-end digital couponing, here's how to get going:

1. Discover any potential software and/or hardware costs from your EPOS provider to handle digital coupons.
2. Call your digital couponing company (e.g. Eagle Eye) to discuss the implementation timeline and integration costs.
3. Build the bake business case and get internal sign off.
4. If an EPOS software update was needed, test the software update and roll out to your estate.
5. Integrate the couponing software with your IT and web teams.
6. Educate your marketing teams on using the system.
7. Let store staff know about the coupons.

Digital Coupons For FMCG Brands

Here's how it works.

If you are an FMCG brand…

(Deep breath)

It's complicated, okay.

Hopefully, by the time you're reading this, it's slightly less complicated.

But it probably won't be.

End-to-end digital couponing is also the Holy Grail for FMCG brands, but there are a number of barriers in the way.

In order for a digital coupon to work in a wide range of grocers across the country, you need the retailers' involvement. Because you need to get the stores to accept a digital coupon, redeem it and organise the discount to be applied to the shoppers' bills and then make sure the financials between you and the retailer are sorted out.

To do that, there are two main stumbling blocks:

1. Scanning through glass.
   Only around 10-15% of the Big 4 grocers' estates EPOS systems can scan a mobile screen to read a digital coupon. This means that if FMCG brands runs digital coupons, the majority will have to be redeemed in supermarkets by typing in the unique code into the tills. This could cause frustration from staff and resistance from retailers. As the main supermarkets upgrade their EPOS systems for those that can scan through glass, this problem will resolve. But that might well take 5 to 10 years.

2. Retail coupons
   In order for a grocer's EPOS system to accept the coupon, it would need to be set up on the system. That means it needs to be a retailer coupon, not just a brand coupon. This adds an extra layer of implementation.

There are some workarounds to making digital couponing a reality that are starting to come to market. Companies such as Eagle Eye and Coupons.com are starting to find ways to manage the process of digital coupon handling.

Eagle Eye, for example, is able to issues and validate digital coupons in real time in One Stop stores and now in Asda. Coke and Greggs have run successful digital couponing campaigns with Eagle Eye and One Stop, while in 2016, Eagle Eye ran the first trial digital couponing promotion with Nicotinell, with vouchers redeemed at till in Asda stores. We suggest you get in touch with Eagle Eye and Coupons.com to investigate further.

Should Your FMCG Brand Build Its Own E-commerce Websites?

One major problem for brands is that four main grocers own the relationship with their shoppers. This is true in physical retail as much as it is in online retail. And the grocers make good money from charging FMCG brands to create in-store POS to create some kind of stand out.

Beyond shelf talkers and online ads, the FMCG brand can do little to control how much prime space it is given in store. (Of course, there are financial arrangements that secure better space from a strategic perspective too, and this involves either becoming a category leader, or by agreeing to frequent price discounting).

All of these options to gain stand out in physical stores are expensive and at the whim of the grocers. At any time, a retailer can run a range review and decide that the brand disappears from a large number of stores. It can have a devastating effect on brands when it happens.

And online sales aren't much better. If you want to stand out on the endless shelves of the dotcom grocers, you better be prepared to pay for banner ads, Favourite Interrupters and shop-in-shops, all the time eating into your profit margin on the extra sales this media generates.

The problem is that the grocers are a major sales channel. FMCG brands are dependent on them.

So what can be done?

Well, you could start your own e-commerce site.

You might well be thinking that no one wants to buy just your products from your own standalone e-commerce website. And I get that concern. You may well be right.

But I'm not suggesting you start your own e-commerce website to replace the grocers. I'm suggesting you being your own site to spread the risk – even if it's only to reduce your dependency on the Big 4 by half a per cent.

The role of your e-commerce store probably won't be to engage with every segment of your shoppers. Your want to make your store the go-to place for people who love your brand – frequent purchasers and loyal customers.

The objective is to move a heavy user into a super-heavy user, and to get loyal customers to become loyal advocates.

Here are a few thoughts of what you can do with your own e-commerce site:

1. Trial new products before your launch them to the wider public. If your fans love them and tell other people about them, you know you've got a great product to launch. If your biggest fans don't love them, you've just saved yourself a whole lot of wasted marketing money launching a flop.

2. Offer amazing service and personalised products. Go above and beyond to help your loyal customers with their every desire. Be generous with your help and watch them repay you with positive word of mouth. Then go on to offer them personalised products they can't get elsewhere. Lindt offers the ability to build your own chocolate box. But you could go further. What if I can personalise the packaging? What if I can buy products I can't get anywhere else? What if I can buy unusual flavours of food products, or even create my own? What if you run a crowd-sourced poll or contest to create a new SKU?

3. Deliver your brand anywhere, anytime. Okay, this may be a little sophisticated for some of us, but it's a great way to impress your loyal fans with brand experiences they will rave about for a long time to come. What if they can buy from your e-commerce site and have your products delivered to wherever they are within one hour? You're in the park with your friends enjoying the sun and the beer is running low. You tap a couple of buttons on your app and arrange delivery of a hamper of beer and snacks, brought by courier to your exact location.

Step 4 Key Points:
Jail-Breaking E-Commerce: Freeing Sales From Its Desktop Prison

• Don't think of e-commerce that happens on a website on a computer. Mobile transactions on apps and sites are increasingly important, as is *add to cart* technology, turning any digital marketing assets into checkouts.

• Just because a customer researches online doesn't mean he will buy online. E-commerce is not just a sales channel for your business, but also a supporting channel to drive physical store sales. And vice versa.

• Click & Collect is a key driver of traffic to physical stores.

• Shoppers expect e-commerce to be convenient and easy with free and fast delivery. Fast is starting to mean same-day, not next week.

• There is opportunity for entrepreneurial food brands to investigate e-commerce growth categories, such as takeaway delivery, vegetable and grocery box delivery, and recipe kit boxes.

• Digital coupons can drive physical and digital sales and provide the Holy Grail – the ability to track behaviour from awareness through to sale.

Jobs To Be Done:

• Review your e-commerce sales with your team, grouping sales into four groups:

1. Breakout hits, e.g. a two-litre bottle of Coca Cola

2. Very popular core products, e.g. Heinz Spaghetti Hoops

3. Niche products with good sales, e.g. Vitamin Water; energy bars; soya milk

4. A long tail of products, with low sales of each SKU, e.g. ironing water; Booja Booja ice cream; Fentiman's Cream Soda

Eighty per cent of sales will likely come from 1 and 2, but buckets 3 and 4 will drive market share.

• Shoppers want retailers to provide great experiences, but often e-commerce sites fail at that. Review with your team how you can deliver a better experience with 1) Personalised shelves and content; 2) Online chat; 3) Personalised products.

• Review the key e-commerce opportunities with your team: distributed e-commerce; digital coupons; owned e-commerce sites.

Step 5:

Post-Purchase: Creating Digital Advocates

Sriracha is the best hot sauce in the world.

It's true! If you don't believe me, you're wrong. You're probably one of those people who insist on eating ketchup.

Huy Fong, the makers of sriracha produce over a tonne of the sauce every hour. That's 20 million bottles a year.

If you like sriracha, you love sriracha.

The man behind sriracha arrived from Vietnam to the US in the 1980s and was frustrated there was no decent hot sauce to put in his pho soup. So he set about making one in order to make sure the Asian community in Los Angeles had a hot sauce.

He never started the company to get rich, and even today says he has no list of where is sauce if being sold – he knows he has 10 distributors he has dealt with for over 10 years. Because sriracha uses fresh chilies – not dried, like other sauces – they can only make hot sauce as fast as they can grow and harvest chilli. The chilli harvest lasts 10 weeks, during which time 45 million kilograms are picked.

The company's focus is on production and making an excellent, consistent product. They leave the marketing up to the fans, who advocate for the sauce, ask their local store if they sell it, and make all kinds of fan merchandise from clothes to tattoos to recipe books.

1,315 sriracha fans recently funded a Kickstarter project with $21,009 to make a documentary movie about the 33-year-old sauce from South-East Asia.

The people who funded that movie are far from crazy. Like me, they know it's the best sauce in the world and want to share the joy of a sauce made from fresh (not cooked) chillies and garlic, with everyone they meet.

To Huy Fong, their sauce fans are better than any marketing campaign. Because they don't run any marketing campaigns. In the entire company history, Huy Fong has invested precisely zero in marketing and advertising.

In a world of battling for supermarket shelf space and endless content marketing, have an advertising budget of zero seems unlikely. But it's true.

The cost of not marketing or advertising the sauce is that it has taken 20-odd years of the lifetime of the sauce to reach mainstream consciousness. But when it did, the buzz has been entirely word of mouth.

There are two interesting lessons to be learned from sriracha's overnight 33-year success story.

- Marketing pounds can speed up awareness of a product but it far from guarantees success
- Fans delivering word of mouth marketing is the most persuasive kind

There's a third lesson that should hardly need saying, but is perhaps overlooked in a world of rapid fire new product developments, and designing products based on continual focus group research: A really good product is the best way to generate word-of-mouth.

The First Rule Of Loyalty

What's most surprising about the sriracha story is how uncommon it is. Many brand marketers believe people love their brand much more than they do. The first rule of loyalty is making sure you have your distribution right, so you appear on shelves when people are looking for your product. Some brand marketers believe that a large majority of sales come from people who love their brand and would happily advocate for it. But the truth is that most people pick a brand they are familiar with because it's in front of them.

The same goes for retailers. Many retail marketers believe that people love their brand and that's why they choose them. But the first rule to being selected is about location. If you have the right location, you'll get footfall. If you have a nationwide distribution of stores with great locations, you'll get selected. But that's not the same as having a loyal army of brand advocates.

Take coffee shops as an example. Starbucks worked hard to create a new kind of environment – the third place. It was neither work nor home. It was a bit like sitting in your own living room, but with barista-quality coffee. Of course, the model has changed the High Street forever. Many people love Starbucks. Many people hate Starbucks. And when you have a brand that divides people, it's a sign that some people are fervent loyalists. They'll advocate for your brand.

But take Starbucks' UK competitors. Do people love them enough to create an army of advocates? Think about Costa Coffee. How many people do you know who *love* Costa? Who would tell you about their pumpkin spiced lattes or frappuccinos over the water cooler at work? What about Café Nero? Does their offering and experience generate not just brand recognition and footfall, but a fervent love for the brand?

This is a point you and I might debate, but I would suggest that besides Starbucks, those other brands have significantly fewer advocates. They have reach. They have great locations. They have a decent offering. And they have footfall and a great business. But you'll also find many more people advocating for Starbucks than the other coffee chains.

People may advocate for Innocent smoothies, but do they advocate for other smoothie brands? Samsung has less fervent (crazy?) advocates for its phones and tablets than Apple does.

The first rule to build a foundation for advocacy is for FMCG brands to get good and consistent distribution. It's for retailers to get great locations and coverage of estate. But this does by far guarantee advocacy on its own. To get people to advocate for you, you can't be a good brand – you have to be a great brand that delivers amazing consumer and shopper experiences all the way along the shopper-consumer lifecycle.

Finding The Customer LTV

Tell me… once a shopper has bought your product and the consumer has tried it, what is the most important factor to increasing that shopper/consumer's CLTV – customer lifetime value?

It's the frequency of which they purchase and use the product. (By the way, when I say *frequency*, the word *regularity* might serve better if we're talking about a sofa or a mobile phone rather than a packet of fish fingers. Because, whether we're talking about increasing frequency or locking in regularity, what we're really talking about is forming habits).

To increase frequency we need to build habit-forming shopper behaviour. Which means whether the shopper and the consumer are the same person or a different person, we need to focus on those people when they have a *shopper mindset*.

And this is where the major problem rears its head again when we're talking about smart use of digital shopper marketing. As we've already seen, digital is sometimes only given prominence in only two of the five key phases of the customer lifecycle:

Awareness… and… Loyalty and Advocacy.

Getting Hooked

Loyalty and Advocacy are much more valuable to us from a digital perspective. Because loyalty is all about frequency and regularity, and the eCRM tools we use to drive these phases – email marketing, web, online ads, social media, mobile messaging – are all able to send out regular, frequent and targeted communications. And because communications can be planned in advance, they can be pre-scheduled, making this phase of marketing highly efficient as well as highly measureable.

Nir Eyal, author of *Hooked: How To Build Habit-Forming Products* points of the power of hooked users of a products becoming brand evangelists, because regular users of a product have more opportunities to find and increase the value they find and place in the product.

"Products with higher user engagement have the potential to grow faster than their rivals," says Nir. He uses technology companies as an example, specifically how Facebook leapfrogged MySpace's user base in the early years of social media because Facebook's feature set encouraged regularity of use. "More frequent usage drives more viral growth," he says.

Nir explains the concept of viral cycle time – the time it takes a user to invite another user to the product. Starting with one user, with a viral cycle time of two days, over a period of 20 days you will accumulate 20,470 users. But if you halve that cycle time to one day, you would have over 20 million users. What this example shows us is that a focus on increasing the number of interactions with the shopper/consumer to increase advocacy and decrease the cycle time is a powerful engine to increase sales and customer lifetime value.

So wouldn't it make sense to spend 70% of our focus on digital shopper marketing to increase the Loyalty and Advocacy in existing shoppers, rather than spending 70% of our focus on digital to drive brand awareness?

Now what if we take a leap of faith…. What if we focused on the shopper as much as the consumer through out the whole customer lifecycle? What if we could talk in such a way with our potential shoppers and consumers so that brand awareness, equity, consideration, etc. could all be build in the consumer *and* we talk to them in a shopper mind-set to drive trial, purchase, increased frequency of purchase, increase purchase volume and then frequency, regularity of purchase and advocacy?

What would the effect be then?

So at this point, if you've taken that leap of faith with me, you might be wondering right now: How do we do that? It sounds complicated.

A Simple Advocacy Strategy

We want our existing shoppers to be advocates. Here's how to write a quick and solid advocacy strategy that your team can action...

(Oh, and by the way, remember to stress that advocates are existing customers – people who have already bought stuff from us. We can also put an influencer strategy in place, which might include thought leaders in our field; key opinion leaders such as bloggers; non-purchasing fans; consumers (who are not shoppers); and affiliates. That's a simple game, but a slightly different one. So we're going to focus on shopper advocacy in this chapter).

Here's the strategy:

1. Objectives
2. Identify
3. Actions
4. Incentives
5. Feedback

Let's briefly look at each step in turn:

1. Objectives
This is what purpose you want the advocacy strategy to serve. Is it to reach more of the same existing shoppers? Or to reach new segments? Or to reach out to global markets, perhaps? The advocacy objective needs to be aligned to your brand's business and marketing objectives. And because advocacy works best when it's an *always on* continual scheme, it needs to fit the business objective most clearly. Perhaps you'll flex the specific actions you want the advocates to take depending on the idea behind each campaign. Perhaps not.

2. Identify

Who are going to be your best advocates? This can be easy or hard depending on what metrics and data you have in place already. If you know your shoppers well and have easy methods of identifying the raving fans and setting them apart from the mass of regular shoppers, that's great. This is the part that's most important to get right, to make the follow steps effective, so it's worth getting your CRM agencies involved in this process.

However, if you have little segmented data about your shoppers and want to get started with a test advocacy programme while you build the robust segmentations in your databases, there are some easy places to start to look for your advocates.

– Create your own Net Promoter Score
Create a survey and send it out to your email list. Ask your shoppers to rank your brand or product from 1 to 10 in terms of how much they would recommend it to friends. Collect the data of those who select *9* or *10* – these are your advocates.

– Look for mentions on social media
You can manually search Twitter, Facebook and the rest for mentions of your brand, or you can use social media listening tools such as Radian 6 to search for posts with positive sentiment – people who are saying nice things about you. Drop them a reply to invite them to your advocacy scheme.

– Email advocates
Those people who open almost every email your brand sends – and click the links –are your advocates. Many robust email marketing software tools have sophisticated lead scoring to segment the most active email users on your list from the rest. Create a new segment and invite these to your email list.

Even some of the inexpensive and simple email marketing tools make identifying advocates easy. Mailchimp, for example, gives each person on your list a one to five star rating based on the user's responsiveness to your emails. The five star people are the group to seed your advocacy programme.

3. Actions

Now we need to review the objectives of the advocacy programme and define a list of specific actions we want an advocate to take. If we just assume advocates will say nice things about our retail brand or product if we wand them the odd bit or swag, it makes it impossible to measure the programme or introduce consistency of message. We might want someone to share a specific post on Facebook, or re-tweet something. We might want them to write a blog post or post a product review video on YouTube. We should also think about taking advocacy into the physical world and create quests or missions such as asking people to take a picture of themselves in store, or at home making use of our product, and then post that onto social media channels.

4. Incentives

The great thing about advocates is that they love what you do, so you don't have to necessarily spend vast sums of money on swag bags and booty. Often, product for review is more than enough to keep them engaged – especially if they get to see those products before everyone else and they come with a nice letter telling them how much you value them. Other incentives can be equally (or more) powerful, with little cost. An advocates web portal or Facebook group to connect with one another helps create a deeper connection to the brand and each other. All these quests and missions can be offered in a gamified platform to help members collect badges or rise to the top of the elite group.

5. Feedback

There's value to an advocacy scheme that often lies untapped. Instead of just broadcasting your quests and missions to the advocates, you can make use of the wisdom of the crowd. Who better than your most passionate shoppers and customers to tell you what they want more or less of in future products or promotions, or in-store experiences? Got a new range in R&D? Save yourself money on focus groups and ask for feedback from your advocacy members. And remember to ask them about feedback of the advocacy programme itself. Who better placed to tell you want kind of rewards motivate them most and how they'd most like to talk about your brand?

The Simplest Form of Advocacy – Competitions

The very word *advocacy* sounds off-putting and complicated. Marketers sling around *awareness* all day, everyday, but it's much more rare to see the word *advocacy* on a brief from a client. After all, it's easy to say we made some ads and a lot of people saw them, so we can tick the *awareness* box.

But advocacy demands measurement – how do we know if someone is an advocate for our store or brand? And it would be lame to run ads that said *please tell your friends about this brand*, whereas it's somehow not lame to run ads that say *buy our brand*.

But there is one very simple, very achievable way to drive advocacy without making your brand look like a massive douche – run contests.

Step 1: Pick a contest that is awesome
Experiences trump product prizes. A £10k value gets the best engagement on the prize spend. Giving the winner an element of choice rather than a very specific prize is best. So a really good prize might be: *Win a VIP holiday to the destination of your choice, worth £10,000.* When you create a really awesome competition and promote it through all your available channels, people will tell each other. And in telling each other, they will mention your brand. And when your brand is mentioned in the same remark as a great prize, your brand benefits from the halo effect – people will think more of your brand and feel warm towards it. People will also treat the remark from someone they know as a recommendation.

Step 2: Ask people to share
Run a competition and then ask people to share it and advocate for you. Put posts on Facebook. Send emails that include a *share with a friend* button. In fact, you don't need to actually ask them to share it. You only have to place the contest in a platform that allows sharing. If you run a contest on Facebook and it's a really good contest, people will share it, because some people feel good about sharing, and that Facebook share button is a very simple way of achieving a good deed.

Step 3: BONUS STEP: Make great content
While competitions are the easy way to drive advocacy (and you should do them regularly), you don't even need the pull of a prize to get your biggest fans to advocate for you on a regular basis. You just have to make good stuff and then tell people about it. I know that sounds blindingly obvious, so there are some caveats. Make good stuff. Announce it like a product launch. Create rich-media content that showcases the product in a beautiful way. This is one of the tactics that makes Apple launches so effective.

Here's a really simple example. In 2016, Pret A Manger was talking about increasing its vegetarian choices. They found it was a topic of interest for a passionate segment of its audience. In the image below, all they've done is taken a reasonably nice photo of a new vegetarian menu item and sponsored the update to a target audience on Facebook.

The result? Sixty-seven shares of the image in a couple of hours.

When products are genuinely share-worthy, people will share your content.

Loyalty & Advocacy

Often, advocacy is talked about in the same breathe as loyalty. So much so, that it would be easy to mistake the two as going hand in hand. But of course they don't.

A shopper could have such a good first-time experience of your store that they tell others. They can be advocates at any stage of the consumer-shopper lifecycle. How much they advocate for your brand isn't necessarily tied to how long they've known about the brand, or how long or how frequently they buy from you.

A shopper could be loyal and rarely or never advocate for your brand. I fill the car with petrol every week, but I can't remember ever in my life telling others about a remarkable experience in a petrol station. I tend to go to the same petrol station every time I drive from Brighton to London, but the experience is never particularly remarkable.

(This might be a slightly unfair example, because in this case, I'm not loyal to the particular petrol station because of how good it is, but simply because of its location and convenience. The watch out that can apply to our brands is to consider that many of our shoppers might not be selecting our brands because they love them, but because there's no particular reason to de-select them, or swap to a competitor.)

Using Online Shoppers To Lock In Loyalty

I know we just talked about examples above when advocacy and loyalty don't have to go hand in hand, but of course there are plenty of times when loyalty does drive advocacy. One example is where retailers drive frequency of shops (both in store and online) which, over time, makes them a *John Lewis shopper* or an *Ikea shopper* or a *Sainsbury's shopper* or a *Made.com* shopper.

This move from frequency to loyalty to advocacy can be driven by online shopping. This is an important tactic to consider in a world facing digital disruption, because, at the time of writing, very few brands are taking full advantage of it.

Here's how you can…

Online shopping locks you into a single ecosystem. So whether you're a retailer worrying about the threat of online business or High Street rivals, or a supplier brand worrying that you don't have a direct relationship with shoppers and frustrated with the power of the retailers, e-commerce is a key channel to invest in.

Now, I know my viewpoint above is not the most prevalent one. I know many retailers still view e-commerce as something that is for 10% or 30% of their shoppers, so invest in it accordingly. And many FMCG brands are reluctant to invest in e-commerce direct-to-consumer retailing, citing changes to their supply chain and investment in storage and fulfilment.

But that's not the view that you read of this book, and what an all-round smart integrated marketer wants to have. That *we'll figure out online when we have to approach* is stupid and potentially disastrous for your business.

What you want to do is take tips from Apple and lock in your customers to your ecosystem. With Apple, iPod brought in a whole new audience. iTunes locked them into an ecosystem. When the iPhone came along, Apple made it simple to use your Apple account that you were used to buying music with to buy iPhone apps. The same with the iPad. Now iCloud storage makes use of your Apple account details too. As does Apple TV. As does the Apple Watch. As does Handoff – where you can start a task on Apple software on one device, then switch to another and complete the job, e.g. starting to edit a Keynote presentation on your iMac, then finishing it off on your iPad. What makes Apple doubly clever is they presented more ways to spend money with the company, and they add incremental value to users – the more devices you own, the more you want to stay locked into the Apple ecosystem, so you remain loyal.

We want to engineer some of that lock in with your shoppers.

For retailers, the way to do that is with seamless multi-channel, making sure that ordering online and buying in-store support and complement one another. At a simple level, you can do this by talking about Click & Collect in store.

Here's a photo of a department store clearly signposting its Click & Collect offer. Notice, there's nothing creatively outstanding about the design of the signage, but it is big and bold and grabs attention.

At a more sophisticated level, you can offer loyalty points that stretch across online and in store, or broaden your ecosystem to include your eCRM channels – making sure that every communication in every digital channel and in store gives reasons to lock in shoppers with value.

As an example, let's look at the Big 4 grocers. Loyalty is harder to come by than it used to be. Shopper behaviour is splintering loyalty. As shoppers, we're buying groceries more frequently, with smaller basket spends. The weekly shop isn't quite dead, but it's not the mainstay of grocery retail it once was.

But online grocery shopping is growing steadily. When picking a physical grocery store, shoppers take into account both their retailer of preference and location. They might regularly shop at their second favourite grocer because it's in a convenient location. With online retailing, there doesn't need to be any such compromise. You can choose any grocer that offers Click & Collect. The differences in delivery costs and convenience are minimal, so you might as well buy from whichever store is your favourite.

This thinking could be an opportunity for increased brand loyalty. If you start to use your No.1 preference for online grocery shops, it could condition you to go out of your way to use your preferred choice more often in physical stores.

But there are also dangers. Because delivery options are very similar and online shopping is relatively easy, it also becomes easier to jump around between the grocers, choosing one for online groceries when you're feeling the need to save money, and another when you want to get the best ingredients for a dinner party.

The trick to using online shopping to lock in loyalty to a retail brand is to make sure that the online shopping experience is the best it can be. Is it easy? Does it inspire me? In the case of grocery, the key areas are how easy it is to find the specific products I am looking for, how relevant are the returned search results, and how easy is it to navigate through the endless shelves.

If grocers focus on making the user experience of buying online easy, it will make it enticing for shoppers to return. Those repeat shops reminds the shoppers of what they like about that retailer, as well as reminding them of the ranges and products they like that they can't get at other grocers. This could well go on to influence which physical store(s) they buy their groceries at.

Online shopping should not only focus on average basket spend and as a channel in itself. It should be strategically aligned to the business' strategy to drive shopper loyalty and frequency of purchase.

The grocery retailer that thinks this way will win market share.

And this thinking is not just for the grocers. It's for any retailer that needs to shore up and maintain its market share across both physical retail and online. Your brand may dominate on the High Street or on retail parks, but may face fierce competition from pure e-commerce players. If this is the case, you want to focus on creating a great online user experience to drive brand loyalty across channels.

Winning Loyalty At Home with FMOTs

When we think of loyalty, we might think of our email programme, or a combination of our eCRM activity. We might think about promotional activities at shelf to drive frequency of purchase that we hope drives loyalty. But there's one phase of the shopper-consumer lifecycle that most brands don't even consider when thinking about driving loyalty – the home.

Let's imagine you're selling frozen fish fingers. You might drive brand awareness through your above-the-line media. This is where you have the greatest control over the brand and the story you're selling. You hope that repeated messages over a sustained period of time would drive not just a temporary uplift of sales, but also on-going frequency of purchase. You hope that the frequent purchasing will become an unconscious behaviour – that buying your product or visiting your store will become a habit.

You might run promotional activity in store with the aim of making your store or your brands a more regular choice. You want to be selected on a regular basis, first driven by the promotions and then driven by habit. You hope that people will like your products or your retail experience so much that they then continue to buy from you even when the promotions end.

While the two examples above go about it in different ways, they both aim to create new habits – you want the shopper to select you without thinking. And you want that thinking to happen at an unconscious level, so it's harder for your competitors to lure them away with their advertising and promotions. But if you want to build habits associated with your products, the best place to start is when your shopper is now a consumer – when they are actively using the product.

In the case of fish fingers, the time to drive habits at home is FMOT – the Fridge Moment of Truth. It's Saturday teatime, I've been out with the family playing on the beach, and the kids are hungry and tired. I need a meal they love that's easy to cook – and fast. Like a lot of UK homes, often one of my first choices is fish fingers. Often with peas, often with chips or mash, sometimes with pasta. Always with ketchup and mayonnaise. My five-year-old boy loves fish fingers. Every time we eat out, he chooses fish and chips. I can't go wrong.

As I remove the wet and sandy clothes from the kids and head to the kitchen, I've yet to decide what to make the kids for dinner. I open the fridge and see what's easy, or what leftovers there are I can quickly heat up. I open the freezer to see what we have. There, on the top shelf, are fish fingers. Easy. Simple. Yummy. Reliable. The one meal that's most likely to be eaten when the kids are tired. I grab the fish fingers, and then look for some frozen veg to go with it. Maybe some chips too, or potatoes of some other kinds.

That was the FMOT. It's the moment in the shopper-consumer lifecycle where advertising has no effect. Where the consumer selects the product without the brand-owner's knowledge. And it's where – if you make fish fingers – you want to win if you're going to win shopper loyalty.

Here's how it works for me. See if you can relate to this – especially if you have kids too. Next time I go to do a big shop there are a few particular products on my list to get because we've run out or I've made a mental note to look for them. Then there are a larger number of items that don't even need to go on my list because they are the core staples we eat all the time – they are the ingredients that drive family mealtimes: pasta, sweetcorn, peas, sausages, eggs, milk, bread… and fish fingers. As I reach area of the store where these staples live, I unconsciously pick more off the shelf. I know that most of the time it's an unconscious process because I'll often get home to find out we already had plenty left at home and I didn't need to buy more that week.

The FMOT drives unconscious behaviour in the supermarket. And then I have more of what I usually buy, so it drives more FMOTs. Like a well-used neural pathway, the more I repeat the behaviour, the more the behaviour becomes ingrained. And, almost by accident, I become loyal to the brand.

So the question is: How can I drive this FMOT? How can I lock in this frequency of behaviour at home, to drive frequency of purchase in store?

The way to do that is to divert some of your marketing spend to a remarkable spend. Make sure the experience your consumers have when they use or consume your product is remarkable.

Apple, Birds Eye and Coke Market To You Through Consumer Experience

In Step 3: Hacking The In-Store Experience we talked about the power of experience and how scientific studies show that buying experiences makes people happier than buying things, and that increasingly, people prefer to spend their disposable income on experiences rather than things. In Step 3, we used this insight to talk about the importance of building a great in-store experience. But this insight can also be used to focus your team on designing great experiences for the consumer.

When an Apple fan brings home a new phone and carefully unboxes it, they take great pleasure in that experience. In fact, Steve Jobs and Jonny Ive designed the packaging to provide as much pleasure as possible to contribute to a premium experience. There's no hard-to-remove blister packaging. Boxes slide apart satisfyingly slowly. Cables are meticulously coiled and held together with paper tabs and plastic protects that fit just so. Rumour has it that Ive and Jobs debated the exact length of time it should take a new user to slide the top box off an iPhone.

Birds Eye ran a plates promotion in 2013. From the brief, it was a simple cross-category coupon promotion: Buy three packs of Birds Eye products for £10 to get a free plastic plate for your kid. But Live & Breathe's response to the brief was deceptively clever. Birds Eye wanted to help mums' experience of mealtimes. After all, it's stressful getting your kids to eat their food without getting distracted, deciding they don't want to eat, or painting every surface with food. Birds Eye partnered with children's author Roger McGough to produce beautifully illustrated plates that featured children's stories on them.

The idea was to help mums encourage kids to finish their meals so they could then look at the pictures and read the stories together.

I have five or six of these plates at home, and my kids love them.

Birds Eye created a promotion that drove sales in store by encouraging trial of more products by buying more than their usual list. But even more important than that, they created a way of experiencing their products that was unique and fun. They also found a way of being on the dinner table every day, even if you're not eating Birds Eye products every day. They defined an experience around consumer behaviour that also doubled as a subtle branding exercise – and would likely drive more frequent Freezer Moments of Truths when Birds Eye would get chosen.

Coke – always the innovators – have been experimenting with how to own an experience in someone's home, rather than just have the consumer purchase one of its products. The result of a version of its Keurig Kold machines that dispenses whatever flavours of soda you like. It's like taking one of those soda fountains you see in Burger King and fitting it in your kitchen. Compared with going to the fridge and taking out a cold can of Coke, the Keurig Kold machines create a much more interesting experience of Coca Cola drinks in three ways:

1) It offers you a seemingly endless supply of soda
2) It offers a number of different sodas
3) It allows you to mix those standard sodas to create your own flavours

These three aspects of the experience give a strong sense of freedom of choice – I can drink any flavour I can imagine, whenever I want, at the touch of a button. The Kold machines elevate the role of the consumer to become a collaborator and to choose their own experience of Coca Cola products.

Of course, the consumer has total freedom of choice, as long as the choice is restricted to enjoying Coca Cola products.

There is another clever aspect of encouraging consumers to install soda fountains in their homes, besides the potential to lock in brand choice and drive frequency and loyalty. Coca Cola and Keurig has been experimenting with Wi-Fi connected soda fountains. A benefit for consumers is the possibility of fuss-free re-ordering of soda syrups when the supply runs low. The added benefit to Coke is that they get to learn who is making which sodas and when. They get to acquire huge amounts of valuable consumer behaviour data direct from people's homes – and they get shoppers to pay $300 for the privilege.

The three examples above – Apple, Birds Eye and Coke – show the power of focussing on remarkable experiences in the consumer use phase of the shopper-consumer lifecycle. And while these are standout examples, the opportunity for us as marketers of retail and FMCG brands is to figure out how our product can become less functional and more experiential when people use them. The more time our consumers spend with our products having positive experiences, the more we will drive frequency of use and create loyal advocates of our brands.

How To Do Email Properly

To many, the phrase *eCRM campaign* has become synonymous with *email marketing campaign*. This shortcut in thinking does both a disservice to the power of traditional printed CRM campaigns, and also the value of using other digital channels for CRM: personalised web experiences; targeted social; mobile.

The reason email is seen as central to modern eCRM campaigns is its unique combination of benefits:

• Email marketing is nearly free, once you have an opt-in

• It scales, in both volume and frequency of messages

• We can speak to segments of our audience with targeted messages

• We can personalise emails with first names ("Hi Jenny") and bespoke content generated based on user segmentation, unique data points and customer behaviour pulled from multiple CRM sources.

• Emails can be triggered. New sign up – send an email. Entered a competition – send a follow up sequence. E-commerce cart abandoned – send an offer.

The key role of email marketing is to speak to an existing audience to give advance notice of promotions, products, events and campaigns, using content in those emails to drive frequency of purchase and loyalty.

Email can do a lot of things. But for me, the focus is always on frequency of purchase and loyalty.

Good And Bad Emails

The Bonne Maman email below is a classic example of how to write an email putting brand at the heart of your communication rather than putting the shopper or consumer at the heart. It opens with the brand logo, tells us about a new range, why it's good and where it's sold.

But it completely forgets to involve the viewer in this rather one-sided conversation. It's only broadcasting to the end user, without any attempt to write in an engaging, one-to-one way. You might think emails are a broadcast medium and it's impossible to have a conversation with the viewer. But you want to write emails in such a way that it feels like the reader is engaged in an animated conversation.

You know how they say that everyone's favourite topic is *me*. This email doesn't answer "What's in it for me?" The tone is marketing copyspeak and not how you would talk to a friend. And there's no personalisation, no "Hi Viv…", so the email feels as if it's talked to a large audience, rather than addressing me directly.

Compare Bonne Maman's email with this one from Barack Obama's sent during his second term in office.

While no one is kidding themselves that this email is going out to hundreds of thousands or millions of people, the way the email is structured and the tone of voice makes it feel like it's written by a friend.

The subject line – *Need your help, Viv* – is the kind of line you'd use when emailing a friend of colleague. It offers intrigue. The first paragraph has no preamble. It gets straight down to making a key point and continues the intrigue to keep you reading. The email body builds like a story, with short, punchy paragraphs, written in a way that assumes friendship and common interests. The key to emails that gets readers is to write to someone as if you are talking to a friend down the pub.

This Graze email has an intriguing subject line and headline…

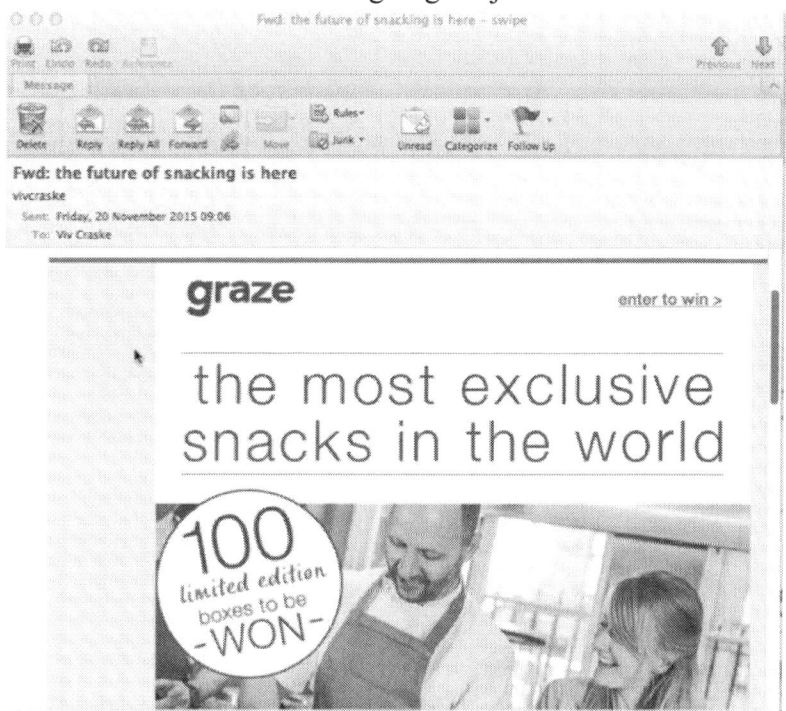

And continues that intrigue with the headline, "the most exclusive snakes in the world". It also convers the *What's in it for me?* question, not just by inviting consumers to join an exclusive club of premium snackers, but with a simple competition, clearly flagged on the screen.

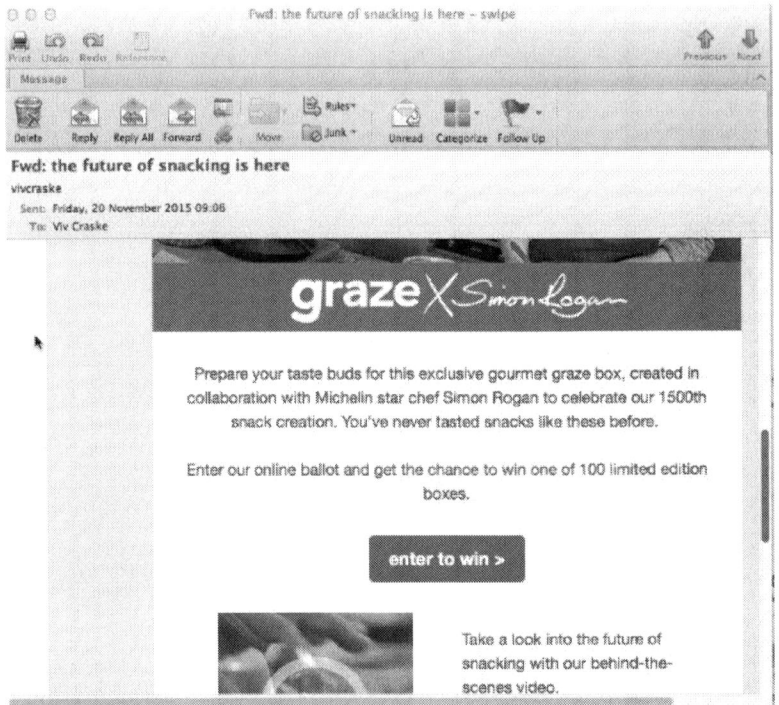

The email continues with a simple layout and clear call-to-action buttons to encourage you to engage and click through to enter the competition.

Because email plays such a key role in eCRM programmes and the ability to drive frequency of purchase and loyalty at little cost, resources should be upweighted and key teams up-skilled to create best-in-class email designs, email content and an inviting tone of voice.

The emails above are simple and don't include any *tricks* to stand out, such as moving images, but they get attention of their audience. Emails need to pass the *meh!* test – do you really want to read on, or do you go "meh" and move on…

Extending The Power of Email

Wouldn't it be nice to double the effectiveness of your email marketing at little extra costs? If you've not already been using Facebook Custom Audiences, you really should. You upload your existing customer email database into Facebook and it matches those email addresses against its users. You can then run ads to your email list on Facebook. You can repeat similar messages to those in your emails, or offer an extra incentive to drive another purchase, such as added value or a discount, only to those already on your email list.

Ratings And Reviews – Getting Shoppers To Do The Hard Work For Us

Wouldn't it be nice if our shoppers did all the hard work for us and turned their digital advocacy into something we can easily point to and say how great we are?

We've already discussed the simple advocacy strategy of asking people to share competitions on Facebook and other social media channels. A more sophisticated but fairly frictionless way of turning happy customers into happy advocates is to aggregate great customer experiences into standardized ratings and reviews. Third-party companies such as TrustPilot allow you to do this.

Here is Harveys Furniture aggregated TrustPilot score. At the time of writing, the retailer isn't placing this score prominently on their website home page, or displaying the score in other channels.

Harveys Furniture reviews

Great **7.9** from 0 - 10

6710 reviews on Trustpilot

However, Harveys does make good use of positive customer posts on its social channels. Here is the retailer re-tweeting a comment on its Twitter account:

Here is a Bensons For Beds customer review. The retailer has a section on its website to display them.

Here, Sofology is using its excellent TrustPilot rating prominently on it's website:

Amazon is the master of using reviews online to drive trust and sales. As we mentioned in an earlier chapter, in 2015 the retailer opened one bookstore in the US as a test store. The retailer made the most of online reviews and ratings by bringing them in store too.

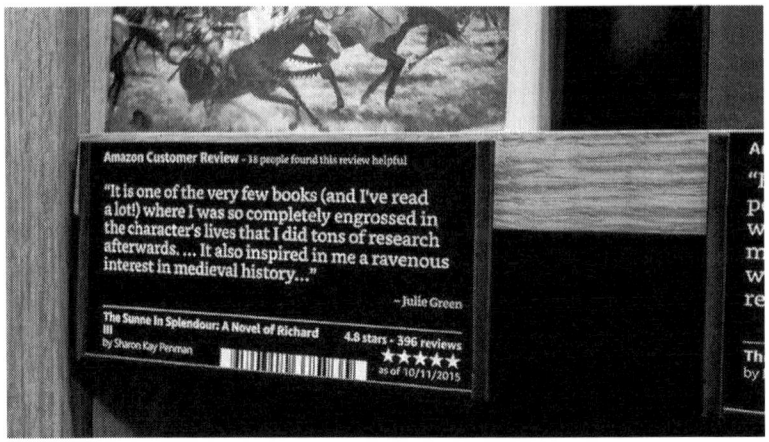

It's also worth reminding us of how retailer Nordstrom easily brings recommendations in store from digital channels. Items that are most pinned on Pinterest are highlighted in store with a simple piece of signage. You might want to steal this idea.

According to a 2013 Forrester Report, 70% of people trust brand recommendations from friends. But only 10% trust advertising. Even if these statistics were only half true, it's worth investing time into designing some tactical uses of online ratings and reviews and social media recommendations to build trust between you and your shoppers.

Getting Advocates To Create Your Content For You

The most sophisticated advocacy strategy involves identifying the best advocates for your brand and consistency communicating with them and encouraging them to promote your products or campaigns. This is often known as a Key Opinion Leader (KOL) strategy.

You might identify key YouTube stars with a large and engaged audience and ask them to talk about your brand in their own style that works for their audience. Or you might find some influential bloggers and send them your product for review. While you're less in control of what people might say about your brand, you get to tap into an existing audience. And because any review or endorsement of your brand comes from a spokesperson who is already trusted by their followers, the return on investment is likely to be high.

Here are some useful questions to ask as you plan your KOL strategy:

1. Have you identified your KOLs?
Sometimes called *KOL mapping*, there are a number of ways to identify your advocates of varying sophistication, from searching on YouTube for the vloggers with the biggest audiences, to social media listening tools to identify those accounts with the most influence.

2. Does your KOL plan need to be for a campaign, or always on?

3. Do you have a team to manage your KOLs?
And who is best to manage that team? PR? Marketing? An agency?

4. How will you make it a valuable two-way relationship?
Will you play your KOLs, or offer rewards in terms of free product, affiliate sales or entry into competitions?

Step 5 Key Points:
Post-Purchase: Creating Digital Advocates

• The first rule of loyalty is making sure you have your distribution right, so you appear on shelves when people are looking for your product.

• Consumers who use a product more frequently are more likely to get *hooked*. So it makes sense to focus on increasing frequency of use.

• Use competitions that can be shared on social media sites to drive simple word-of-mouth advocacy.

• Online shopping can be use to lock in loyalty to an omni-channel brand.

• Use always on email marketing to drive frequency of purchase and loyalty. Write emails as if you're talking to a friend, and personalise them.

• Collate online ratings and reviews and use them in your marketing materials.

Jobs To Be Done:

• Review your distribution. Ask your team how it can be improved.

• Design your advocacy strategy with your team. What's the objective? Who are your advocates? What actions do we want them to do? Who will we incentivise?

• Review your competitions, ratings and reviews and any key opinion leader activity. What's working? What can be improved? What can become always on?

• Ask your agency to review your email marketing – the strategy, communications plan; segmentation, content, and tone of voice. Review the open rates and click through rates.

Step 6:

Hacking The Brief

Having reached this far in the book, you're probably questioning some of the legacy ways in which your team plan strategy and execute campaigns. The biggest challenge is delivering integrated marketing to help retail and FMCG brands survive digital disruption is the brief. Whether that brief is an internal work to help your team execute against (even if it's a few bulletpoints in an email) or whether that's a brief you send out to your creative agency, this is the starting point for helping your extended team understand what's required to create campaigns that work well.

Here's the main problem. Most briefs are lazy. Ninety per cent of the ones I see say they want awareness and sales, without any recognition that those are two different parts of the consumer-shopper lifecycle with different marketing needs. Sure, you can have awareness and sales, but you need to appreciate that you'll want two different strategies for that with two sets of outputs. Most briefs don't get this.

I think it's because many brief writers do not have a clear understanding of the consumer-shopper lifecycle or the psychological basis of successful marketing. Or perhaps the write is pressed for time and hopes the person reading it will figure out what the job to be done really is. The problem is that often the receivers of the brief will not come back to the brief writer and tell them it doesn't make sense. And so what you end up with is a solution that tries to solve the problem that the person who needs to deliver on the brief thinks is needed, but without 100% focusing on the best solution to the problem.

There's a whole book that could be written at this point about how marketing practices and dogma need to change for a digitally disrupted world, but I know that what you want is a solution you can implement with your team now, not another book to read.

What's The Problem?

Three key legacy issues stop us from focusing maximising the impact of always on digital platforms:

1. Ignoring the consumer-shopper lifcycle and shopper mindsets

2. Incorrect budget allocations

3. Siloing of departments

The Five-Minute Brief Fix

The simple solution to the problem above is to make one small change to your briefs to get your teams to incorporate a digitally disrupted world.

At the end of the brief, include a section that asks: "What is the digital solution to this problem?"

And make sure that the response you get includes this answer. What's interesting is to see if the team that responds just adds in a few more digital touchpoints than usual, or if they consider the question at a higher level and question how else this brief might be solved if digital marketing best practice is involved.

Re-Thinking The Budgets

It might well be worth re-considering your usual marketing spend and advertising budget allocation with the arguments in this book front of mind. The way we used to do things was to reach a large audience by buying large TV, print and radio audiences. But can digital heavily supplement or replace those traditional mediums?

While digital media does allow you to measure some metrics such as engagement or click-throughs, at a simple level, the one thing we can definitely measure with digital media is reach. We can reach a large targeted audience. And we can probably reach that large target audience at a very competitive price compared with TV, radio and print. So what if we just treat digital media as another above-the-line channel? Forget everything digital media could do when you're planning to drive awareness for a campaign, and focus on reach.

Note: You want to verify that the audience quality is the same or better than your existing media buying options. After that, re-allocating spend towards digital becomes a no-brainer. It's cheaper. It's targeted. It's flexible. You can change your campaign targeting and creative at a moment's notice. What's not to love about that?

Campaigns Vs Always On

The other problem with campaigns is that they tend to focus around a specific creative territory or set of assets. The novelty of those assets drives awareness of the campaign.

But is this always the best approach? When the creative changes frequently it can make it hard for consumer and shoppers to remember your brand. Some brands are famous for having advertising campaigns that have a consistency of messaging, rather than jump from wildly different campaign creative year to year.

Remember when Birds Eye introduced Clarence The Bear? The chances are, the answer is 'no'. If I ask you which person or character you most associate with Birds Eye, who would you say? Captain Birdeye, right? The jolly ship's captain with a big beard. Yet, for a few years recently, Birds Eye dropped the captain from its campaigns in favour of a small white bear. Sure he was cute, but he wasn't the captain. The cost and time to associate the frozen foods brand to another character was huge. And the cost to re-introduce the captain recently is also huge.

While we need campaigns for new product launches, and we might want to create a tweaked set of campaign assets for a new Christmas campaign or a new back-to-school campaign, I do wonder if every single campaign needs to re-think existing campaign assets.

The opportunity of using an 'always on' digital approach is that we don't necessarily need to focus so much on generating new campaign assets. Instead, we can deliver consistently and regularly and frequently the brand values, and benefits of the product, in digital channels. Why say new things all the time about your brand, when you can spend the money you save on new creative on digital ad spend instead?

Your Research Probably Sucks

Sorry to break it to you like this, but your brand research might not be as robust and up to date and you'd like it to be. In fact, there's a good chance that when an agency asks you for it, it's not something the brand has thought much about for a while.

If I'm wrong, I'm sorry. And if you email me a contemporaneous piece of research about your brand that doesn't have any glaring holes in it, I'll very happily buy you a pint and apologise.

There are often two problems with research that brands supplier to agencies to help them define the audience of their communications:

1. The segmentation is out of date
2. The segmentation reflects who you would like to buy your products rather than who is actually buying your products

We can use digital research tools to remedy both of these problems.

I was told a too-familiar story by a friend who was working on a well-known food brand. The brand's supporting documentation point to one of the key audience segments as "sophisticated diners" who regular held dinner parties, looked to top chefs and restaurants for recipe inspirations, and only bought the best ingredients to go with this brand.

The reality was that the brand may once have had this positioning, but the brand's success had led to a wide mainstream adoption, meaning that the characters in Eastenders were just as likely to cook with this brand as anyone.

The problem was that the brand denied the existence of these consumers and shoppers. It wasn't that there was a strategic decision not to market to them. It was a complete denial that the brand's end consumers weren't entirely sophisticated diners. This caused a problem between various departments and agencies that each tried to skew the conversation and the briefs in the direction that made the most sense to them. It was messy and frustrating.

Of course, a great brand knows exactly who its audience is and does not deny them, even if they do have an ideal audience segment in the mix. A great brand dives deep into the most currently available research to identify new audiences and sub-audiences, the media landscape they inhabit and the changing shopper and consumer behaviour they display. They make sense of all of this within the current macro-trends, and they provide a pithy summary of these findings within a brief, rather than copying and pasting in audience info from previous briefs.

Social media listening is a great tool to check and validate previous audience segmentation and to discover and new audiences. There are many different types of social media listening tools on the market that deliver different outputs, but my favourites are Affinio and Audiense, because they help identify new audiences – or tribes, as Affinio calls them.

Brands are missing out on an up-to-the minute source of consumer insight that can make campaign planning across all channels more effective. Tools like Affinio and Audiense help brands remain relevant. The tool taps into the interests and passion points of online audiences relevant to your brand and tells us what they're currently talking about.

In the following example from Affinio, we used customer segments from Twitter followers to create tribes of different sizes to help us build a social landscape of the food delivery sector. We mapped 55,861 Twitter fans of one or more of these brands: Deliveroo, Just Eat, HubBub, Eat First and Hungry Horse.

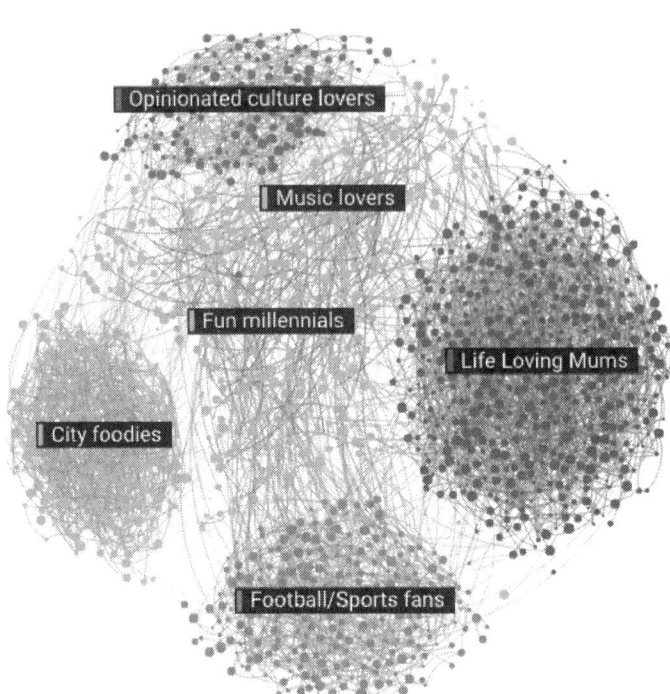

The image shows us how these tribes are self-organised consumer segments, based around common interests and attributes, such as sport of family life. You'll notice the tribes in the images are different sizes and have varying numbers of connections both within a tribe and to other tribes. This shows you the size of each tribes and how much the tribe members talk within a tribe and to other tribes.

In the above example of food delivery fans, the Fun Millennials and Music Lovers are highly connected and engage with each other, but Footfall/Sport Fans and City Foodies are less well-connected to other tribes.

There's a very good chance that if you use a tool like Affinio or Audiense, that you'll discover new audience segments that are not prominent in your existing shopper and consumer profiles. This is because: 1) these tribes are creating over the previous monthly, so are extremely current; 2) this audience is based on audience interests and connectedness, rather than starting with demographic data, then overlaying interests.

Even if using a tool like this only goes to validate your existing audience segmentation, the sizes of these tribes and how inter-and intra-connected they are should overlay new insight on top of your ones.

Once you have taken a detailed look into the insights these tribes provide, it's worth asking your team to consider how we can create bespoke creative, or even campaigns, to talk to individual tribes. You might even ask what you can do to get these tribes talking about your brand in order to drive word of mouth advocacy to other people like them.

Test & Learn, Not Create & Execute

Here's a normal briefing process:

1. Brand writes brief
2. Agency create outputs
3. Brand uses assets

Sometimes, there is a fourth step:

Brand reports back on campaign metrics to agency.

But it's not a step that happens often. Which is crazy when you think about it. If an agency is any good it will provide research and look at previously similar campaigns to identify what's working well right now.

But what if we could test out the creative ideas the agency produces before they are run as campaign assets...?

Sure, there have been elements of testing and validating marketing ideas for as long as there has been marketing. But qualitative researching is often mis-leading because the audience size isn't big enough, and qualitative research can be expensive and time consuming.

Digital marketing tools offer a solution that can be added into briefs and added into the agency-client process to create better ads.

Here are 2 examples:

1. Test TV on YouTube

Shoot more than one version of the same TV ad – such as different endings, different beginnings, or different call to actions. Instead of sending one TV ad to air based purely on creative approval, run both ads on YouTube to existing fans or as targeted ads. See which one performs best in terms of views or click throughs. Based on this real data, pick with TV ad to run.

(Extra tip: YouTube videos come with analytics that show you how engaged your audience is second by second. Look at this graph to figure out what grabs attention the most and what gets viewers tuning out.)

2. Test Creative On Facebook

If you are choosing between two or more creative routes for a campaign, why not let your existing fans tell you what they like…? Create an image showing two options: A and B and run this image as a promoted post to your existing Facebook fans. See which one gets the most votes.

Note: Most brands won't do this because they are either nervous of giving away this much control to shoppers, or they worry about what competitors or industry peers will make of this level of transparency. While these concerns are valid, I think they are out-weighed by the value of asking real people help pick what they like most and reducing the risk of a campaign bombing because it's been created by a small number of people only taking feedback from each other.

(Extra tip: For brands comfortable with transparency, you can look at asking your audience on Facebook (or email) for their opinions on products as well as marketing. Why not crowdsource opinion of planned packaging changes or new product development. Personally I think it's more insane for a brand to develop a new product and only to test it with a few focus groups before a multi-million pound launch, than it is to reveal a little of the inner company workings to fans of the brand an potentially avoid an expensive failure.

Ask For Better Briefs

Agencies are expert at writing briefs. It's the difference between a good and a mediocre brief that steers to the creative team to produce great rather than ok work.

Retailers and brands are often not as good at writing briefs. That's just how it is.

Ask your agency on every single brief: "How can this brief me better?"

Ask you agency to show you their internal brief and ask them what they added and took away. Ask them why they wrote the campaign proposition they did.

Ask your agency to run a brief-writing workshop for your team. Focus on getting better at briefs if you want better results.

Step 6 Key Points: Hacking The Brief

• Most briefs are lazy and don't offer a clear objective, falling back on asking for "awareness and sales".

• For more integrated briefs, write at the end of the brief: "What is the digital solution to this problem?"

• Allocating more money to digital ad spend over traditional media can often reach a larger audience for less money.

• Audience segmentation is often dated. Use social media listening to identify new audience tribes.

• You can use digital channels as a test and learn resource before you release your marketing campaigns into the world. Use YouTube to test TV ads and Facebook fans to choose campaign designs.

Jobs To Be Done:

• Review your brief-writing process for internal briefs and agencies. What can be improved? What can be done to get more integrated/digital responses?

• Review allocation of media budgets and compare media efficiency to see if digital channels can be more cost effective than some other channels.

• Review existing audience research and segmentation to see if you can benefit from social media listening.

Step 7:

Six Blind Men And An Elephant: Killing The Silos And Dogma That Cause Your Team To Fail

Imagine that one day you meet a group of blind men who have discovered an elephant. Each blind man is touching a different part of the elephant and the group is trying to agree on what they are touching might be and look like.

One blind man who is touching the elephant's leg says it feels like a tree trunk. Another man is touching the elephant's side and says that what he is touching feels nothing like a tree trunk. It feels much more like a tall, flat wall. A third man is at the back end of the elephant and has caught hold of the animal's tail. He says that what he's touching feels like a rope, nothing like a tree trunk or a wall. Confused and irritated with each other, they argue and disagree for some time.

Because we're watching the entire group grapple with the elephant, we can see that each man's experience is right. And it's only when the bling men start listening to each other that they can then begin to see the full picture and describe the animal based on their collective experience.

In our industry, the elephant in the room is that integrating digital marketing is a lot like the blind men feeling the elephant – people with only one piece of the puzzle think their experience is the whole puzzle and not just one piece.

Ditching The Silos

Imagine you are an alien who is visiting your marketing team for the day to try to understand what is happening. He asks you what everyone does.

"Well, this is Dave; he's from our above-the-line agency. And this is Polly; she's from our shopper marketing team. Will is from our e-commerce team. And Sarah works alongside Will in the digital/e-commerce team and looks after email marketing and eCRM."

"And what's the purpose of digital in this campaign?" the alien asks (because he's very smart and we've prepped him in advance).

"Awareness through online ads," says Dave, the ATL guy.

"I'm not sure if there is a role," says Polly. "Maybe some online ads to drive to our e-commerce store."

"Definitely, Polly," says Will. "But digital in this campaign is all about conversion to online orders. Online shopping is increasing – soon it will be at least as important as physical sales, so we need to treat it seriously."

"But right now, sales in physical stores are more important than e-com," says Polly. "So digital isn't a key role in the brief I've been given, Will. At least, that's my understanding."

"I think we need to check our email schedule," says Sarah, "to make sure we're not bombarding the list. Reading through everything I've seen about this campaign, you want emails for campaign awareness, then there's follow-up emails from the on-pack promotion."

"But we also have a load of loyalty club emails going out in the same time period. The loyalty emails are more important than anything else, so maybe we'll just send one email about the campaign a couple of days before the TV campaign runs."

Are there elements of this pretend conversation that you recognise? Doesn't it seem a lot like the blind men with the elephant? Like the blind men, Dave, Polly, Will and Sarah are all 'right' when you consider their own channel and responsibility on its own. Digital can fulfil all the roles they're talking about. And some of these choices add more noise for the shopper or may blow the focus or may take resources and focus away from the main thrust of the campaign.

The trick is to get Dave, Polly, Will and Sarah to see beyond their responsibilities and the myopic view it creates. Don't reward and measure each of them by fulfilling their channel roles, but by creating a best-in-class digital campaign that asks the bigger question: How can integrated digital marketing drive more sales, more efficiently and with less friction?

Let's remember that to the shopper and consumer, they do not have their experiences of the brand put neatly into boxes offered up by business silos. They just experience their communications they happen to see, in whichever order is driven by design or luck. And it's the combination of comms that will influence them through the consumer-shopper lifecycle.

This doesn't mean that digital channels shouldn't have a role. They should have a very clear role. And by defining that role for the brand, and tweaking it for each campaign, allows the team to work towards a common goal.

Getting People To Work Together

When I talk about ditching the silos within brands and retailers and agencies, the number of people who nod along is growing. Most of us see the logic that myopic campaign planning and execution doesn't make sense. But that acknowledgment that departments cause marketing inefficiency does not say anything about a team's intention to make changes or work together more efficiently in the future.

So how do we encourage teams to work together on a campaign?

The answer: scrum teams.

Scrum is a term that evolved from lean project management practices, and evokes the rugby scrum where a team comes together at regular intervals within the game to re-group, huddle, adjust strategy and work together.

There's three ways of creating scrum teams that will work for your organisation.

1. Get the team to work together for the duration of the project

If the campaign is big and important enough and the company and workload is flexible enough, you can move your cross-discipline team to a new area in the office. Sit them together until the job is done. Get your brand manager, your marketing exec and your digital team member in one place. Get them to plan together and execute together. The physical proximity will encourage communication and agreement towards the overall campaign objectives, and will no doubt encourage more creative thinking on how to achieve it.

2. Get the team together for regular WIPs

Make sure the team kick off the project together and set in the schedule at the outset of the project the on-going Work In Progress meeting. Agencies are often better at this than brands, so ask your agencies how this works for them. Meetings should have a defined purpose rather than general discussion.

Project management software should be used to keep everyone up to date with the project progress. WIPs should be used to make decisions or sell in more complex ideas into the wider team to garner support and make sure everyone is bought into the ideas before they move forward.

Make sure you involve your agencies at every stage of the project and treat each agency as important as the other. Invite the below-the-line agency and the digital agency (and any specialist agencies) to the same campaign kickoff meeting as the lead creative agency. You might ask your creative agency to write the brief and provide visual stimuli to help define the project.

Time To Build A Growth Hacking Team

Growth hacking is a terrible term that is easy to disparage. But the value of growth hacking can be huge.

What is it? Growth hacking is as much a mind-set as a process.

It says that we start with the product and make it as great as possible.

It says that we look at existing consumers and shoppers to see how we can encourage them to drive frequency and market share growth through advocacy.

It doesn't follow the received marketing dogma of how a campaign should work and looks for the most cost-effective and efficient way of driving sales.

Often growth hackers don't think that the answer is an expensive creative campaign. Which, of course, can rub some traditional marketers the wrong way. To growth hackers, data is king. A campaign creative is good if the data says it's good. It doesn't matter if the agency executive creative director and the brand CMO loves the idea.

"Let's test and see," is their mantra.

And even better, "Let's split test and see."

You want to create a growth hacking team because they do not think in silos. If they were blind men examining an elephant, they would examine the tail and say, "I have a theory that this is a rope. How can we test that?" If their assumption is wrong, they keep examining the elephant, find the side and say, "I think this is a wall. How can we test?" And they keep going in small test-and-learn cycles. The outcome of each cycle feeds into the next test. So, after a couple of tests, a growth hacker would say, "Our assumptions about what we're feeling individually are wrong. How can we get a better view of what this thing is?"

They quickly create theories, test them quickly and use this insight to feed into the next test. They do not accept all of the assumptions and plough all their money and resources into a campaign without testing the assumptions that worry them.

This approach may well be new to you, but it will also save you a lot of money. Growth hackers can test their assumptions in digital channels with simple creative assets and low-cost campaigns. The results of a few rounds of testing will give you a greater understanding over which of your marketing assumptions were right and which need to be changed. This feedback can go into the brief you give your creative agency to deliver the next big campaign.

To create a growth hacker team, you need people on your team who have practiced growth hacking before, or are willing to learn. Get them to read Ryan Holiday's book *Growth Hacker Marketing*. Add in a forward-thinking product/retail staff member and a head of innovation. And set them the brief. See what they come back with before you set the task to your usual internal team or your creative agency.

Get Trained

Sometimes people think that training means something is wrong. But what training means to me is that the people we're training are worthy of investment. Team members who like learning will learn of their own accord. They will read LinkedIn articles and blogs and white papers and books and listen to audiobooks on their commute. If you give them a login to an online learning platform like Lynda.com, they'll use it. If you give them training, they will be enthusiastic.

To the people who aren't proactive learners or are suspicious of training, we can talk to them about how we can help them. Here's the problem…

Many clients I've worked with are asked to do more with less. Maybe budgets are tightly controlled. Maybe they have less staff on their team than they would like.

But even if the team is resourced well, because the world of consumers and shoppers has changed, and the number of available marketing channels and touchpoints have increased, the world is more complicated than ever. It takes more time to deliver a good campaign when you know a lot about each channel. If you are not up to date with what's possible and what's working now, it can be tough. Many people I speak to are overwhelmed with things they should know.

And because the world is changing constantly, training needs to be regular and on-going. Think *kaizen* – constant, never-ending improvement. Most agencies will be more than happy to train your team, run a workshop or be paid a retainer to produce a monthly or quarterly innovation report that cuts through the noise to tell your team what's working right, not what's relevant to them.

When people don't know enough to do their own job at an 8/10 level or enough, it's a problem. When they don't have time to understand other people's jobs and knowledge as well… that's when silos happen.

Silos: Organisation Dogma + Limited Resources + Lack of Knowledge

The easiest way to cut the silos is to feed teams with knowledge.

Too Many Stakeholders

Because human beings are social creatures, groups of people generally want to get on (I know if you've ever had to deal with an HR issue, this may be hard to believe, but stick with me…).

And because we want to get on, science shows that decisions made by a group of people tend towards the mean opinion.

This is a huge problem for creative teams and creative marketers. If you've ever worked in a creative agency, or if you ask your agency colleagues, they will tell you that the best ideas are most often discounted in the initial stage of a brief or pitch.

Some ideas will be discounted because they are not on brief or on brand, but just as often, they will be discounted because one of the stakeholders doesn't quite get it, or has questions, or has a personal preference for another idea that is easier to get.

The problem is that *easy to get* often equals *safe*, and in a world of increasing noise and decreasing cut-through of any one marketing message, *safe* equals *losing money*.

These are some of the things I have heard over the years:

"I don't like purple, so we can't have that."
"I'm not on social media, so I don't get any of this."
"I don't click on online ads, so this won't work."

But, of course, it's not about what one person thinks. It's about what's going to work for the audience. And while we all have our experience and acumen, we also have opinions that are rooted in outdated ideas, personal preferences and political decisions.

Don't believe me? Let's try this out…

Here's an image from Obama's website homepage during his presidential campaign in 2008. In the main area of the image, Obama's marketing team split tested a number of different options – plain black and white images, coloured images, and videos.

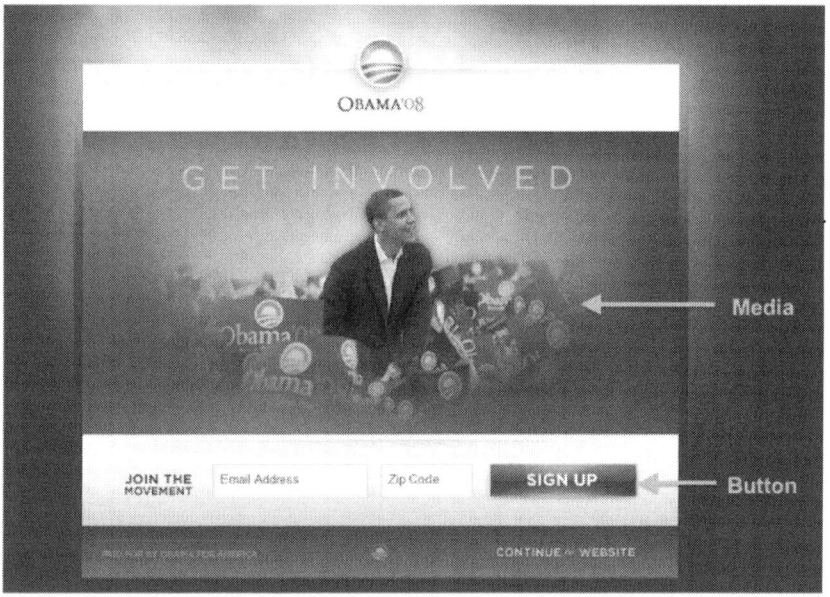

The page encouraged people to sign up and join his campaign. The call to action was an email opt-in and a signup button. The marketing team split tested different buttons too:

Which was the best-converting sign up button, do you think? I would have guessed *Sign Up* or *Sign Up Now*. How about you?

The winner was *Learn More*.

How about the winning image or video?

As a marketer, I find myself saying things like, "Video is more engaging than images," and most of the time, saying that colour images stand out over black and white images hardly needs saying. That's why four-colour newspaper ads are sold for more than black and white.

Obama's team also tested six different options for the image above the email opt-in box. Three are shown below. Which of these three do you think helped produce the best opt-in rate?

You can watch all six here, including the videos: https://www.flickr.com//photos/optimizely/sets/72157625300462626/show/

Option 1: Black and white photo:

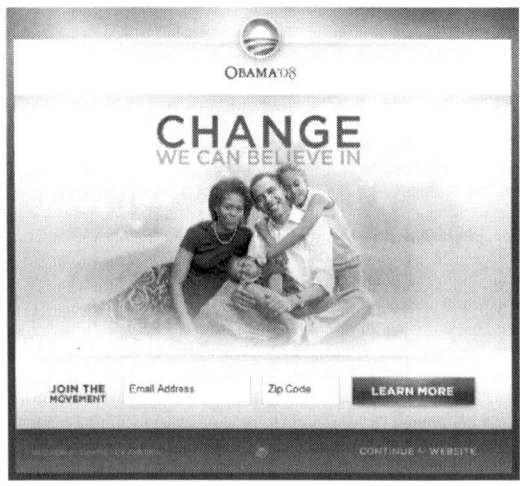

Option 2: Colour photo:

Option 3: Colour video:

Which did you guess?

My guess based on previous experience was the video. The rule I used to talk about without question was: video outperforms flat images.

If you guessed either the video or the colour photo, you might be surprised to learn that the winner of the test was the black and white photo.

This image with the *Learn More* call to action was the winning variation for the campaign and it had a sign-up rate of 11.6%. The original page had a sign-up rate of 8.26%. That's an improvement of 40.6%.

Ten million people signed up on the opt-in page during the campaign. If the team had not split tested the buttons and image options, the original page would have produced only 7.12 million signups. That's a difference of 2,880,000 email addresses.

The campaign team then followed up with emails, which they split tested. These emails persuaded a whopping 10% of those signing up to volunteer. The campaign team also asked for donations using split tested emails to drive the best results, delivering an average opt-in of $21 donations, delivering $60 million in additional donations. This was the first political campaign where more donations came from the electorate than from large business donors and private donors, and it's all thanks to split testing the campaign messaging to drive the best results.

What the example above proves, is that assumptions can be wrong. It also proves that data is king. And while stakeholders are important to get on board with campaign strategy and creative, it's important to create a culture where if we're not sure about an idea, we aim to test it rather than get rid of it because one of the stakeholders isn't sure of it.

Internal teams and agencies can create what they think are great designs, but we need to test those assumptions. And as each of us has our own assumptions and creative likes and preferences, the more stakeholders involved in a campaign, the greater the chance that we create work that tends towards the middle-ground. We are also more likely to rule out quirky, strange and outlandish ideas. That's why we celebrate truly innovate ideas that work, such as Compare The Meercat or 3's Dancing Pony.

The more stakeholders we have in the process, the bigger this problem becomes. Unless we figure out how to ask the data which idea is good and which is bad.

Budget For Data Acquisition

Byron Sharp is Professor of Marketing Science at the University of South Australia, known for his work on loyalty programs. He's a marketing academic who has written over 100 conference papers and journal articles. He likes to take the marketing assumptions that most of us employ every day and check to see if they are really true or just received wisdom. He put many of his most important findings in his 2010 book *How Brands Grow*.

One surprising finding came out of years of research and studying the data across many categories and large retail and FMCG firms. Professor Sharp found that brands don't increase market share by targeting existing core users.

I know! I had to read the statement twice when I first saw it in his book.

Sharp found that successful brands need to reach people who are not in their core target markets to grow market share. The majority of successful brands' sales come from *light buyers*. These are the people who buy relatively infrequently. And because they buy infrequently, these are the people us marketers often overlook. When you look at the audience targeting section on most briefs, the focus for a campaign is to target existing core audience segments. This might be a good idea to slow lapsing buyers or to drive frequency through use of new purchase and consumers' occasions or to drive awareness of a new product or retail offering. But if you want to grow market share long term, we need to talk to the light buyers who we rarely target in our communications.

Digital is a great set of channels to use to grow this audience of repertoire buyers, because we can target them, media buying is cost effective, and we can track their behaviour in our CRM.

The easiest place to start looking for light buyers is to create a segment of email users who have not opened an email of ours in the last three months. We can create a campaign of a series of emails just for this group. What offer, help and advice, or engaging content might we send to them to re-engage them in the hope of driving sales?

If your CRM database also holds physical sales or online sales data, you can also cut the data to find light buyers – those who have not purchased in the last 12 months (or whatever time frame is appropriate for your business).

But to truly grow our brands by focusing on light buyers, we need to find more light buyers. Whether you use offline or online targeting tools to build an audience profile, you'll then need to advertise to them and send them to an opt-in page where we show them a great offer (that we split test!) in order to encourage them to give us their email address or phone number.

Once we have their details, we can create a follow up sequence of communications in order to encourage them to make a purchase. (Note: Don't hound these people with communications after the initial on-boarding sequence of comms – these are light buyers, remember, so we need to communicate with them appropriately if we want them to remain in our CRM database and our area of influence).

This process of building light buyers should be always on. Because some buyers also stop buying our products and services, we need to replace them on an on-going basis. And if we're serious about taking Byron Sharp's advice about brand growth through light buyers, we need to create a process that talks to their potential buyers more often than in campaign bursts.

In order to make this always on process acquisition process work, the strategy and associated costs need to be signed off by the business at the highest level. We need to discover the CPA – cost per acquisition – of these light buyers. We need to decide how many we can afford to add each month, tied to the business growth objectives. Then we need to have a line in the budget for this growth.

Depending on your viewpoint, the last paragraph will be either obvious or quite radical. But it's also a really, really good idea. Campaigns are expensive and don't necessarily drive brand growth over time. Engaging light buyers does.

Step 7 Key Points:
Six Blind Men And An Elephant: Killing The Silos And Dogma That Cause Your Team To Fail

• Integrating digital marketing is like blind men feeling the elephant – they think their experience is the whole animal. Overly focusing on specific business silo jobs to be done without considering the overall business and marketing objectives creates confusion and inferior results.

• Silos: Organisation Dogma + Limited Resources + Lack of Knowledge

• Create scrum teams to work on key marketing campaigns, either by seating teams together for the duration of the project or bringing all stakeholders together for frequent work in progress discussions. Project management software can keep all team members up to date in real time.

• Create a growth hacking team to provide a new approach to key briefs.

• Plan for on-going digital training for your teams. Think *kaizen* – constant, never-ending improvement. The easiest way to cut the silos is to feed teams with knowledge.

• Reduce the number of project stakeholders and answer "I don't like it" and "I'm not sure" with "Let's split test it and see."

• Marketing research show that brands don't increase market share by targeting existing core users. The majority of successful brands' sales come from people who buy relatively infrequently. Use always on digital campaigns to acquire these people.

Jobs To Be Done:

• Review your organizational ways of working with your team and review your organizational structure with an outside consultant.

• Create scrum teams or run a trial of scrum thinking on a project. Review (or implement) project management software use.

• Ask your team to learn about growth hacking approaches.

• Ask your agency to provide regular digital/innovation updates and trainings.

• Review if your briefs' objectives are in line with Professor Byron Sharp's brand growth findings.

Amazon's Killer Terminators

When I was a kid, Mum would take my sister and I to the market on Saturday morning. There were two things I liked the most.

The fishmonger who sold fish that you could get in Tesco – dabs were my favourite, and we'd eat them – together as a family – on Saturday evening while watching bad quiz shows on ITV.

I also loved the dodgy market traders who sold all sorts of rubbish in mock auctions. They sell a mystery cardboard box for £2 to one shopper and it would turn out to contain a microwave. The market seller would then announce that he had 10 other boxes as valuable as that, for £20 each, and hands in the crowd would fly up to secure one of the last deals. Invariably, those further mystery boxes contained a set of Teflon saucepans, the only mystery being how the wonky handles stayed long enough for you to carry them to your car.

We went to the market because it sold different stuff from our big Tesco (the same Tesco at the bottom of town where I worked when I was 16). We got our fish and dodgy saucepans and some fruit and veg at the market, then we'd go to Tesco to get the majority of the weekly shop. If we were feeling lazy or in need of a treat, we'd buy a couple of microwaveable ready meals – Tesco had just started selling a range, and it was a real treat, without the higher cost of buying takeaway.

On occasion, after we'd loaded up the boot of the car, Mum would drive us from the bottom of town to Yeovil's newly built Quedam shopping centre to Bejam. To younger readers, Bejam was the same as Iceland, but without the luxury of prawn rings and Kerry Katona adverts. There, we'd stock up on freezer foods, again often focusing on things that made meal times easy, such as pizza, or occasional treats like spiral fries and ice cream.

When Mum went shopping it was always a weekly shop.

If you didn't do a proper weekly shop, it was a real pain, because supermarket store opening times didn't allow for much time to shop outside weekday work hours. If you ran out of an essential in the week, like bread or milk, I might be sent down the road to the local corner store, where, besides Heinz beans and Green Giant sweet corn, the majority of branded goods were the low-cost Happy Shopper range.

The only other time the local corner shop got our business was on my walk home from school, perhaps buying a sherbet Dib Dab with my friends, or when we were 15 and 16, perhaps a can of Top Deck shandy to look cool.

Despite all the talk of microwaveable ready meals and chips and ice cream, we were a pretty healthy family. The vast majority of nights, Mum cooked from scratch. Rice with fish and vegetables, pasta, chicken casserole, kedgeree. Most often with a small side salad, which was a combination of little gen lettuce, celery, cucumber and orange pieces, for some reason!

Takeaways were rare treats. Eating out options were fewer than today and coffee café culture had yet to arrive in the UK, so eating out was limited to Sunday family pub lunches, or a café at a park or zoo or gardens we'd visit at the weekend.

Able & Cole had only just launched, so the concept of a weekly delivered veg box was an alien one in Somerset. As were farmer's markets. Of course, there was no online delivery. And Jamie Oliver had yet to wrestle food cookery TV from Delia Smith and Keith Floyd.

Cooking and eating was simple. It happened at a dinner table or in front of the TV.

Shopping for food was simpler. It happened weekly. People were loyal to one supermarket, even before Tesco Clubcard was launched in 1995.

And because cooking and eating and grocery shopping was predictable, it made marketing predictable.

It seems quaint now in a world of emoji-ordered takeaways, soon-to-be drone deliveries, weekly delivered recipe kits with just the right amount of each ingredient, and a Starbucks, Pret, Costa and Itsu on every High Street tempting me to eat and go and avoid cooking. And let's not forget the *local* versions of Tesco and Sainsbury on every High Street as well as the symbol retailers such as Nisa and Spar. And while the story above is my childhood, it seems like it happened to someone else. It seems such an odd world to have lived in with limited choice. Somehow, less fun, less technicolour and less sensual. The pleasure of being able to eat whatever I want, whenever I want was absent.

Some statistics for you…

In 1965, people spent 62 minutes preparing dinner. In 2015, it's 32 minutes on average [source: Kantar World Panel].

Large format grocery stores are expected to reduce their share of shops by 2.9% in the next five years, while convenience stores saw and increase in shops by 27.4% in the last five years. In that same five-year period, the number of people saying they shop at a discounter has risen from 3% to 15%.

And with 2 hours 26 minutes daily spent on mobiles, compared with 3 hours 12 minutes spent watching TV [source: eMarketer, April 2015], the chance of having dinner accompanied by a mobile or iPad is pretty high – no wonder we love Instagramming our food!

People want whatever they want, when they want it, where they want it, at the right price and to feel good about whatever they buy. The job of marketing at and in store, whether that's a brick and mortar one or somewhere digital, is to make me think it will be easy and enjoyable to buy from you... and then make it enjoyable and easy to buy.

Amazon gets this. Its mission statement is to be *Earth's most customer-centric company*.

That's the part of the mission statement that people remember, but the full statement is of particular interest to us as FMCG and retail marketers:

We seek to be Earth's most customer-centric company for four primary customer sets: consumers, sellers, enterprises and content creators.

Amazon wants to be *the everything store* for our shoppers. And it wants to be the most popular store for FMCG brands and branded goods companies to work with. To understand this mission statement in practice, let's take a look at some of Amazon's shopping-related activities, at the time of writing:

• Amazon has launched same-day grocery delivery service Amazon Fresh in the UK.

• Amazon is planning to offer home delivery recipe kits – a Gousto or Hello Fresh killer – through its Amazon Fresh service.

• Amazon offers one-hour delivery on products from electronics to milk in key UK cities through Amazon Prime Now.

• Amazon already sells its own branded electronics. It's experimented with selling own brand nappies and is in talks with white-labelled CPG companies in the US to create a number of branded goods ranges.

• Amazon Subscribe & Save allows you to sign up for automated repeat purchases on its site in return for a discount.

• Amazon launched its first physical store – a bookshop – in Seattle.

• The US Federal Aviation Administration granted Amazon permission to begin US testing of a prototype drone delivery system in 2015.

• Amazon Dash buttons allow you to program a button you stick in your kitchen (or wherever you want) to re-order any item with one push of a button. Out of dishwasher tablets? Just press the button and Amazon orders it for you. A handheld device, confusingly also called Dash, allows you to scan the barcode of any object and add it to your Amazon shopping cart.

• Amazon's Echo is an ambient computer – a small cylinder that sits in your room waiting for your voice command. For now, it can play music and tell you information on Wikipedia. But it could easily order items for you on Amazon soon.

• Amazon has build a cyborg – metal endoskeleton over living tissue. They roam the streets, forcing you to switch your High Street and online shopping to Amazon or they will terminate you. They cannot be killed. They cannot be stopped.

Okay, the last one might be made up. Maybe we're not quite going to be overrun by Amazon's killer Terminators just yet. And no one is forcing us to use the company that in 2014 increased its cash reserves by 68% to £5.90 billion. But the endless waves of innovation to increasing shopping categories, combined with its insane cash reserves (compare Unilever's 1.9 billion cash reserves in 2014) makes Amazon a serious threat to all of us involved in retail.

Here's the bottom line: Amazon wants to replace the supermarket AND compete with your FMCG brands, and charge you to play in their world. They want to compete with your retail store and they will deliver faster and cheaper items than you probably can. They have more money and clout to do this than any current UK supermarket or brand powerhouse, or UK retailer.

And if it's not Amazon's killer terminators forcing shoppers to brand switch, there's plenty of market innovation coming from start-ups who have no understanding of how retail *should* be done – with none of the legacy costs and dogmatic thinking either.

In 2015, Ocado's market valuation was around £2 billion. Ocado worked hard for that valuation being a grocery delivery innovator. Then along comes a company like Instacart in the US, which was just three years old in 2015 and employed 100 people. They use shoppers to select your grocery items in store then have them delivered to you within an hour. Based on the investment rounds at that time, the company was worth $2 billion.

Predicting The Future

Every industry has faced, is facing, or is about to face digital disruption. Digital is often the means that allows innovation to march forward more quickly than ever before, catching traditional *safe* businesses unaware. Hello Blockbusters and BHS and Woolworths and Austin Reed.

iTunes disrupted the record industry.

Google Maps disrupted the mapping industry and created a new one.

Netflix is disrupting TV.

Uber is disrupting the taxi industry worldwide.

Airbnb is disrupting the hotel business.

Tesla is using technology not just to disrupt how cars are made, but how cars are sold too.

PayPal is disrupting online payment merchants.

Innovation is just change that delivers increased value. The value may be to the end user or to a customer in the supply chain. But at each and every stage, it's digital that is allowing speedy disruption.

According to Dear Media Consulting, the next industries about to be disrupted from 2015 onwards are: healthcare, finance, education and retail.

Food-tech, for example, is a hot area for venture capital investment right now, with investments going to start-ups operating at every point in the industry vertical: farming, manufacture, supply chain, marketing, delivery, consumption.

So just how scared should we be? How soon before Jeff Bezos announces those killer terminators delivering your one-hour deliveries?

One man has an impressive track record of predicting the future of technological and scientific innovation and change. Ray Kurzweil is a futurist who has been predicting the future with uncanny accuracy for 30 years. In 1990, he predicted a computer would beat a human at chess by 1998. It happened in 1997. He predicted mainstream Wi-Fi by 2010, and he predicted voice commands for computers by 2009… and, well, we have Siri…

Take a look at the graph below that shows Kurzweil's predictions of increasing computing power. By the slope of the curve, it's easy to see that if his predictions are correct, human beings are only just beginning to harness the power of computing.

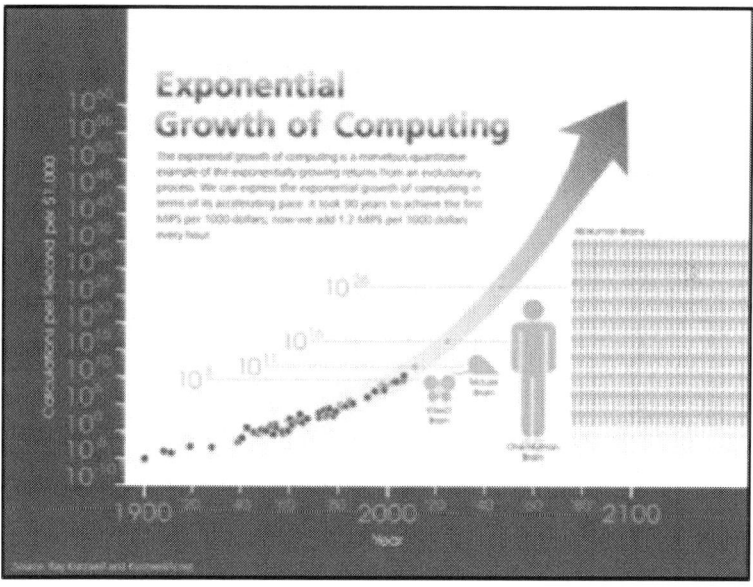

In fact, Ray has some very disconcerting predictions.

By 2029, robots will be able to outsmart us.

By 2050, computers will be smarter than the entire human race.

Of course, Kurzweil might be wrong. Part of me is excited about this strange possible future, and part of me is scared. And I think that's an entirely appropriate response.

Now let's put those predictions about computer power into our context. When computers are as smart as a mouse, what are the likely changes to what marketing looks like? It's hard to guess, but it's easy to extrapolate out by a few years.

Flexible 1mm thin screens are coming to market soon. E-paper screens that can be placed on any product or surface are coming. Perhaps our signage in and out of store and our product packaging will incorporate digital elements.

CRM is likely to become predictive rather than reactive. Media buying is likely to go the same way. We'll be able to guess which groups of people are likely in market and looking to find out more about our brand, or buy it.

In the rest of the chapter I make three specific predictions about where marketing and the retail industry is destined. These predictions are by no means a definitive list, not perhaps the most likely major changes we'll see in the next five years. They are more like mini essays offered here as thought starters to encourage you to start to predict where your industry niche or category is going.

We might not be able to predict the future, but we can at least ask some useful *What if?* questions that will help us prepare for whatever is round the corner.

Prediction 1: AI and Bots Will Disrupt Marketing Again

The emergence of bots on Facebook (see image below), Twitter and Kik will re-ignite the debate around whether technology helps us connect to people or separates us from them.

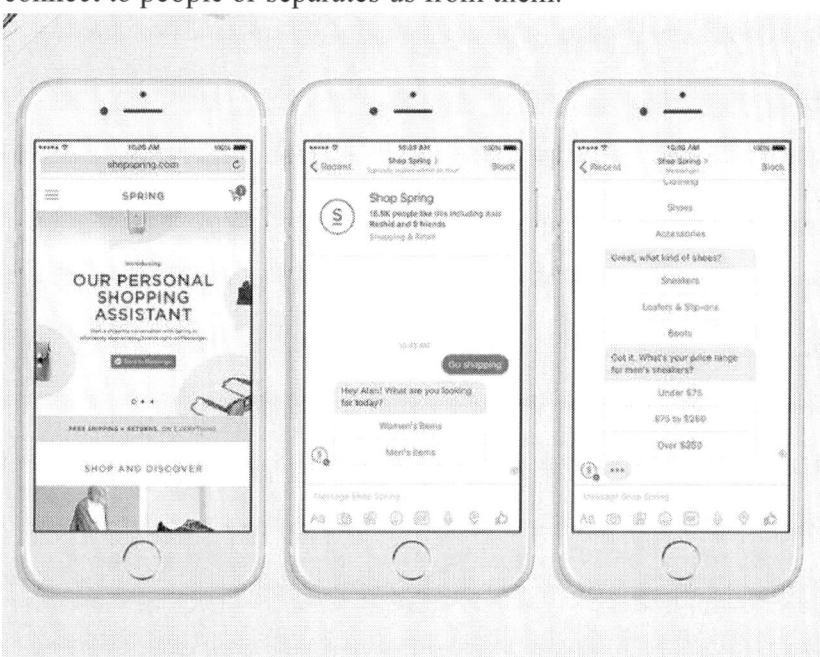

When a group of teenagers are not talking to each other, but instead staring at their phones, some would say that there's a loss of human connection.

But to us marketers, the arrival of bots provides a different problem. What does our customer service efforts look like when we are able to provide AI-based help and solutions in real time? And as Facebook encourages bots to become a concierge and recommendation service, what does that mean for our marketing plans?

There's now an app for everything. I don't think you need a bot for everything. But for some things, bots will be much more impactful. Customer service centres will use bots and humans together to solve problems. The test of whether these bots are successful will be whether people are more or less irritated being served by an AI quickly, or waiting in a call centre queue to talk to a real human – who may or may not be any better at fixing problems.

The role of bots in 2017 is as a digital friend getting stuff done that takes up too much of our time and thoughts. Done well, bots will free us up to do other things.

When the AIs move from app-based bots to ambient computers like Amazon's Dash, it means we will be able to drive awareness of our products and brands directly into people's homes. Creating a new marketing and sales channel that goes straight into people's home will be a powerful tool, but it also throws up a huge problem. If someone is searching for a lawnmowers for examples and they ask their Facebook bot for a recommendation, which suggests Brand X, which is then bought with a single click, that's great from Brand X, but what about Brands A, B and C who never even got a chance to make themselves known to the shopper? In a world where anything can be bought instantly on the back of a recommendation algorithm, it might become much more important to be the best or the cheapest, rather than to expect marketing communications to attach sizzle to the steak.

Prediction 2: Meat Without Animals Is The Future

Cruelty-free meat, lab-grown burgers, cultured meat, test tube meatballs...

Every week there's a new article heralding the arrival of cellular agriculture – taking a few cells from an animal, then growing them up in a lab, over and over again to make meat products that no longer require an animal.

The small handful of cellular agriculture research companies and start-ups must be very pleased with the (mostly) positive coverage. There's Modern Meadow in Brooklyn creating cultured leather and lab-grown meat. Memphis Meats and Sergey Brin-funded Mosa Meats are also working on lab-grown meat. There's Clara Foods in San Francisco making egg whites in the lab, and Muufri that is making animal-free milk.

The last two companies have been supported by industry body and non-profit New Harvest, which helps fund emerging cellular agriculture businesses. All of these companies are getting rave reviews from the likes of *Fortune* and *Wired* and even *The Daily Mail*.

But here's the problem: The good press will not last.

As products start to come to market in the next couple of years, the popular press will start to play on people fears. They'll be discussion of Frankenstein foods.

If we're not careful, the companies listed above will be discussed alongside Monsanto, with all the ill-deserved attendant damning press and social media rage. The very people who should be the first buyers of these new animal-free products – those who care about animal welfare, the environment and sustainable food production – will turn against these products and decry them for not being *real* food, and how they may be dangerous to eat.

This narrative happened for GMO foods.

It will happen with cellular agriculture. Unless we act now.

Cellular agriculture is fast becoming a water-cooler topic, with strong opinions being formed.

Taking any new product to market is expensive with a high failure rate. We need consumer opinion to be on the side of these science-based companies, to help them plant their seeds in fertile ground.

But here's the good news...

We can identify a good approach to talking about cellular agriculture that drives acceptance of scientific principles and mass-market consumption of products.

To change the world's eating habits, we need a strategic approach to find the right message to win the hearts and minds of global consumers...

Here's the problem: None of the companies above are hiring chief marketing officers. They are hiring researchers because they are perhaps two to three years away from commercialising their work. But now is exactly when we need to start planning product launches and influencing the discussion.

Cellular agriculture has such huge promise to feed the world without cruelty, and to positively impact the environmental impact of global food production. Let's have the foresight to start shaping the conversation now, so that these new foods can go to market and be accepted on our dinner plates.

The time to start planning is now...

Prediction 3: Someone Will Disrupt Grocery With a Killer Food App

Six out of ten people say they do not have a useful grocery app on their phone (Source: IGD, 2014).

There is a huge opportunity wide open for a retailer or a technology company to build that useful food app that people love.

You might think that only 40% of people have a useful grocery app because online shopping hasn't reached a higher penetration yet. But you have to ask, "Why not?" The same survey showed that 72% of people have useful online shopping apps in other categories.

At the moment, people are using grocery apps in spite of their poor quality. People want convenience and ease of shop and recipe inspiration. They would love to have a great food app if someone made one. The public is just waiting for it to be built.

Uber is a great transport app that no one was waiting for.

Deliveroo is a great takeaway delivery app no one was waiting for.

Instagram was the new social media app no one was waiting for.

Each of these stand-out examples created a new premium app experience out of a supposedly saturated, staid and commoditised market.

If you build it, they will come.

Of course there are food apps available. They're just not that great.

Someone needs to make a great one.

I want a great one. And I'm sure I'm not alone.

The apps from the big grocers take online shopping on a desktop and shift that experience to an app – with lots of scrolling and endless shelves.

They are not inspiring. They are functional. Except that they are not *that* functional, because they're not that easy to use.

Apps like Hello Fresh and Gousto and Marks & Spencer aim to inspire with beautiful photography. But they fail to capitalise on that fleeting inspiration. Those apps are missing out on a way of getting people hooked and making them open the app again and again.

Offer apps like Shopitize and Checkout Smart provide value and go some way to hook users. But they tend to hook bargain hunters and coupon clippers. And there are many more people willing to get hooked on a killer food app.

In no particular order, here's what a killer food app could do:

• Inspire me with beautiful photography

• Use AI and big data to suggest new recipes from my usual buys

• Allow me to create multiple shopping lists for different types of shops: big weekly shop, store cupboard staples, weekend treats, dinner parties, kids meals, favourite meals, etc.

• Offer one-hour delivery and same-day delivery, not just one-hour slots

• Deliver grocery ingredients and meal kits and ready meals and takeaways – if I love a meal and I buy into the brand, why can't a company like Birds Eye disrupt the market and supply the food in the right format for *all* the different occasions I want to eat it?

• Offers that inspire me to try new meals or add a twist to old ones, rather that just shout about NPDs or aim to force a brand switch

• A social network of people like me I can share my meals with – it works for Instagram

• A way of gamifying the experience to make it fun. Rewards schemes are out-of-date and boring

• A user experience that feels natural. Tinder turned the tedious business of searching for dates from endless profiles into the mobile-friendly *swipe right to Like*. Grabble is taking that idea into fashion while ASOS snoozes. What's the grocery app equivalent of great UX?

• The content in my app should not look like the content in my friend's app. Recently my vegetarian friend was sent an email by Waitrose suggesting lamb for Easter. Why didn't Waitrose see that she never buys meat and personalise the content accordingly?

This is an open request: Please someone make a great grocery app.

The focus needs to be on ease of use first, then inspiration.

The world needs a great food app right now. Whoever creates it will disrupt the market and steal market share.

I look forward to using it.

The More Things Change, The More They Stay The Same

As retail and brand marketers, we have a choice to make. Do we believe in the High Street has a cornerstone in the future of retail, or do we swallow the popular narrative that the High Street is doomed and that everyone is shopping online?

Retail is at a crossroads. One path leads to our brands thriving on a busy High Street. The other could lead to the creation of a series of ghost retail towns, with stickers in the shop windows inviting us to shop online or visit our store at the retail park.

The truth is this: the High Street is more important than ever before.

In a 2015 Future Of The High Street survey that Live & Breathe conducted, 1,000 UK shoppers were asked which store they wanted to bring back to the High Street. Sixty-five per cent of those shoppers said they wanted Woolworths to return to the High Street (increasing to 72% of women). Fourteen per cent wanted Blockbuster to return.

Shoppers still want something from the physical retailers. As humans, we crave human connection. We like to interact with people in person. Physical retail gives us something we're not ready to give up.

The High Street versus online shopping argument is a false dichotomy. People are shopping more and more online *and* they are still shopping on the High Street. Humans are social creatures conditioned by consumerism – we want to have somewhere to go with friends and family at the weekend to hang out together. That's where the High Street (and out-of-town retail parks and leisure destinations) comes in. While the world is changing at a rapid pace, some things stay the same.

The High Street is evolving by changing shopping behaviour around which channels they shop in and how they use technology. The economy grew just 0.5% in Q3 2015, and just 2.2% growth is expected in 2016.

The challenge for retail moving forwards is how to grow in a cautious economy while innovating in response to changing shopping behaviour. The State of Retail 2016 Report from creative agency Live & Breathe shows retailers what shoppers really want – and what they don't in fact care about.

The results of the survey show online shopping increasing at a rapid pace. Thirty-five per cent of respondents said they visited the High Street much less or a little less in 2015. It would be easy to initially read this data as further evidence of a decline in physical retail.

But 65% of respondents stated they visited the High Street either as often in 2015, or a little more or much more.

The popular narrative is that the High Street is in desperate, endless decline, with empty streets turning our town centres into ghost towns. Shoppers are at home, shopping online, only leaving their homes to pick up takeaways or to visit artisan bakeries.

But this belief holds as much weight as a 5p carrier bag. Of course, it's not our fault that we are led to conclude the High Street is in its death throes. Online shopping is new and exciting, and Amazon disrupting the grocery market grabs newspaper headlines more easily than a traditional retailer showing steady, organic growth.

The most likely interpretation of the figures in the State of Retail 2016 survey is that e-commerce as a growing channel is attracting a proportion of people's attention, and that the majority of people are visiting both the High Street and retailers' online brands. Multi-channel fragments the shopper journey and, done well, can strengthen the relationship between a particular brand and the shopper.

One clue to this multi-channel success story is in answers to the question: What types of shopping, if any, did you do for the first time in 2015? Thirteen per cent said they bought online for the first time, indicating plenty of growth for the channel. The second highest response was 11% of people using Click & Collect for the first time.

With Click & Collect, e-commerce is giving people more reasons to visit physical retail stores.

The popularity of Click & Collect – starting online and finishing in a physical store – proves that the majority of shoppers want to continue visiting physical stores. They want the best of both worlds: the convenience of online shopping, and the experience of physical retail stores. More than a quarter of respondents (26%) say that Click & Collect is making the High Street better, while around one in five (18%) believe it has *changed the way they shopped* last year. The survey indicates that Click & Collect is a key service that's driving the growth of e-commerce. Twenty-eight per cent of shoppers cite the service as a key element for what's making online retail better overall.

Other indicators of a move towards digital innovation do not show a major swing away from physical retail. Only 6% used a retailer's app for the first time; 8% made their purchase using a mobile phone for the first time (which could include several behaviours including using an app, pure e-commerce and Click & Collect); only 6% used a mobile voucher.

What does this mean for the future?

Multi-channel retailing is increasingly important for shoppers, with a physical retail store at the heart of the shopper experience. When asked, *What's getting better about the High Street?*, twenty-seven per cent of UK shoppers said there is now *more value* in the UK High Street.

The High Street is not doomed. In fact, I believe that online retail brands will start to migrate to the High Street to deliver a multi-channel offering. EBay currently has space in Argos stores. Fashion brand Missguided has concessions spaces in Selfridges. And Amazon has just one physical bookstore at the time of writing, but with rumours that there are many more to follow. I predict that there will be many more online retailers in the next couple of years announcing plans to move onto the High Street and shopping centres.

The High Street will lose retailers too. I predict bank branches will become concessions that appear in retailers such as supermarkets, and branches will disappear considerably. Bookmakers may have a similar fate. Between 60-80% of profits are made online. Physical stores will be for brand awareness and as a mass-communication channel.

We need to stop saying that the changes to the High Street are bad and embrace the very bright and exciting future of the High Street and shopping centres as part of a multichannel, multi-site experience.

As marketers, we need to understand our shopper journeys and the shopper mind-set involved in each channel. Is our shopper visiting an online store on their iPad, filling a moment of boredom and making the most of the convenience of browsing; are they looking for inspiration online or in store; or are they visiting our physical locations as a leisure activity? These mind-sets and behaviours need to be part of a channel-agnostic approach to campaign planning in the future, to make the most of all channels.

Here's to navigating a future of exciting changes and challenges, allowing us to thrive in retail, whether that's with bricks or clicks or virtual reality headsets.

What now?

Firstly, congratulations on finishing this book. Most people say they are committed to improving things or staying relevant, but they are just paying lip service. You didn't do that. You took action. If you have any questions or comments on the content in this book, drop me a line at viv@vivcraske.com or say hello at LinkedIn.

Now I hope that you use this book as a starting point to take action with your teams. You might highlight a paragraph or chapter for discussion with your teams or agencies. Or you might jump to the Jobs To Be Done section to help create an agenda for quarterly review meetings.

While we've covered a lot of detail as well as broad topics in this book, I hope that the overriding message you take away is something like this:

I knew our industry was changing fast and now I know which specific areas to monitor and change in my business to respond to this change.

Remember Charles Darwin… he said that survival of the fittest means that those creatures that are most able to change are the ones who survive. It's not the strongest or the more colourful or the most suited to coping with how things used to be.

So where do you find people who are able to change, and are able to drive change?

One way is to ask new hires and your existing team how they feel about change.

When a big organizational change occurs, are they the ones who focus on complaining, gossiping, asking for endless explanations of what the change means for them and why it occurred and who said what to whom? Or are the change makers the ones who deal with change as it happens and offer to help out, who step outside of their role to fill gaps, and who are always bringing you suggestions for how to improve things and new ideas they've learned about?

The people most able to deal with change are the ones you need on your team.

When hiring, there are three attitudes to change:

1. I do things as I'm told and as they've always been done in this industry or in my firm
2. I have ideas on how things can improve if we made some changes
3. I have my own view – a philosophy – on my area of specialism, and I'm always learning more to re-assess that philosophy

Don't hire many of the 1s. Hire some 2s. Hire 3s in key roles, set them the business challenge and let them get on with it.

As you're reading this book, I hope that you too are a 2 or a 3. If you're not – or rather, if you weren't before – that's not a problem, because you can become one by taking action with the information in this book.

Allow me to end with a silly question I like to ask:

Three monkeys are at the bottom of the tree. Two of them decide to climb the tree. How many are at the bottom of the tree?

The answer of course is: still three.

Deciding to do something and *doing something* are different things. One *can* lead to the other, but in many cases, it doesn't.

Don't be the retailer or brand that is disrupted. Innovate within your own organisation first. Innovation is what you and your company does. Disruption is what other people and companies do to you if you fail to innovate fast enough.

Don't create zebras in supermarkets, or succumb to the Amazon's killer Terminators. Do smooth the path.

Be the monkey at the top of the tree.